How to improve workers' education

How to improve workers' education

A collection of articles on methods and techniques previously published in *Labour Education*

International Labour Office Geneva

Copyright © International Labour Office 1976

Publications of the International Labour Office enjoy copyright under Protocol 2 of the Universal Copyright Convention. Nevertheless, short excerpts from them may be reproduced without authorisation, on condition that the source is indicated. For rights of reproduction or translation, application should be made to the Editorial and Translation Branch, International Labour Office, CH-1211 Geneva 22, Switzerland. The International Labour Office welcomes such applications.

ISBN 92-2-101277-8

First published 1976

The designations employed in ILO publications, which are in conformity with United Nations practice, and the presentation of material therein do not imply the expression of any opinion whatsoever on the part of the International Labour Office concerning the legal status of any country or territory or of its authorities, or concerning the delimitation of its frontiers.
The responsibility for opinions expressed in signed articles, studies and other contributions rests solely with their authors, and publication does not constitute an endorsement by the International Labour Office of the opinions expressed in them.

ILO publications can be obtained through major booksellers or ILO local offices in many countries, or direct from ILO Publications, International Labour Office, CH-1211 Geneva 22, Switzerland. A catalogue or list of new publications will be sent free of charge from the above address.

Printed by Weber, Bienne, Switzerland

CONTENTS

PREFACE

The International Labour Office has prepared this collection of articles, previously published in its bulletin *Labour Education,* to complement and illustrate its manual entitled *Workers' education and its techniques.*

The 20 articles making up the collection provide a detailed description of a wide range of teaching and learning methods and materials that are considered to be specially suited to workers' education. Thus they explain the uses of, for example, discussion groups, reading clubs, role-playing, the labour press, radio and television programmes, tape recorders and projectors, and flipcharts and flannelboards.

Apart from appearing in *Labour Education,* these articles, and others, had also been issued as offprints, in which form they were available in a folder entitled *Methods and techniques of workers' education.* However, as the stock of many of the offprints was used up, rather than reprinting them again separately, it seemed preferable to make a choice of the most pertinent ones and to publish them in one volume where they could be more conveniently referred to.

The likely practical value to workers' education administrators, instructors and students of this volume on its own has been amply demonstrated by the previous demand for the articles included in it, but it should prove of even greater value if read in conjunction with *Workers' education and its techniques* (ISBN 92-2-100195-4), which explains the main current problems and practices in the field of workers' education, paying special attention to means of facilitating the acquiring of knowledge by different types of worker-students, each with their own particular requirements.

Briefing session for group discussion: A model plan

Charles A. ORR
Professor
Roosevelt University (USA)
ILO Workers' Education Expert

In the last number of Labour Education, Professor Orr explained that he had developed a large number of group discussion leaders in Ghana by briefing selected trade union officers for about one-and-a-half hours on the day prior to a course or seminar, and that the majority of these newly trained discussion leaders had succeeded very well. Inasmuch as it is frequently a problem to find qualified leaders for group discussion, we have asked Professor Orr to describe a briefing session as simply as possible.

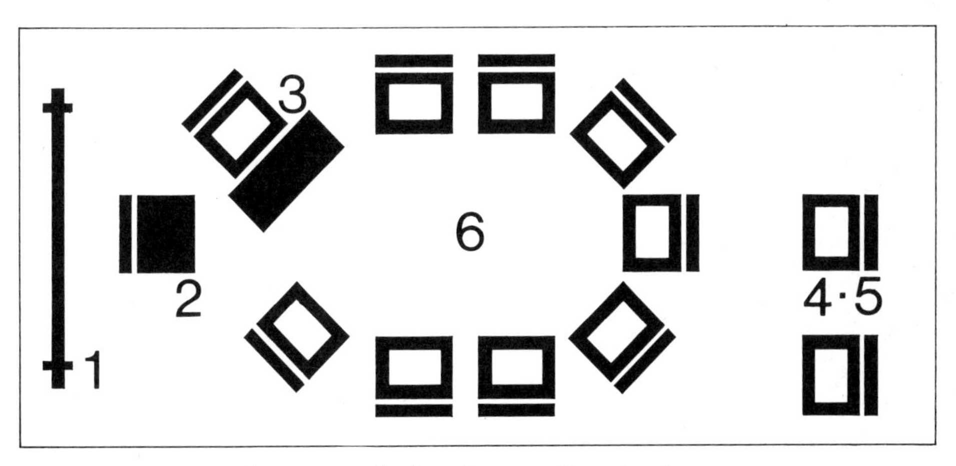

Arrangement of a discussion group. Horseshoe shape:
1. Black-board; 2. Animator; 3. Reporter, having a table available; 4–5. Observers; 6. Participants, their chairs arranged in horseshoe shape

While organising one-day seminars for the Ghana Trades Union Congress in 1968, I had the occasion to brief some 300 group discussion leaders in twelve towns scattered throughout the country. The TUC Regional Secretary was requested to call together a number of promising trainees for a briefing session of at least one hour's duration on the Friday afternoon or evening preceding the Saturday or Sunday seminar. He was instructed to recruit for this purpose regional industrial relations officers of the national unions and as many local branch officers as necessary to bring the number of trainees up to at least one-tenth of the number of participants anticipated for the seminar as a whole.

After being introduced to the assembled trainees, I instructed them in the following way:

•

Tomorrow, from about 8 o'clock in the morning until approximately 4 or 5 in the afternoon, we are going to hold a TUC seminar for the branch officers of this region. This seminar will differ from those that we have had before. For the morning session we are going to divide the participants into a number of discussion groups, with about ten or twelve persons in each group. Everyone will be given a list of questions, and all groups will discuss the same questions. Each group will have a discussion leader and a reporter. We want you to act as the discussion leaders. There may be more of you here than we will need – that depends upon the attendance tomorrow – but those of you who are not called upon to serve as discussion leaders will be assigned as group reporters. Discussion will take place during the morning from about 9 a.m. or whenever the opening ceremonies have been completed, until 12 or 12.30, when lunch is ready to be served. For the afternoon session, Mr. X. will be with us as an expert on the subject under discussion. He will bring us the correct answers.

Now, Mr. Regional Secretary, will you tell us just when and where we are expected to meet tomorrow morning, how long the opening ceremonies with the public officials are likely to take, how much time will remain for group discussion before lunch, how many classrooms are available for group discussion and your estimate of the number of participants we should expect?

Room Arrangements

So you expect about 150 or 200 participants. The principal of the school tells you that eight classrooms are available, including the auditorium. Perhaps we can find some hallways or verandahs which are suitable for discussion groups, should we decide to have more than eight. Will you be able to take me over to the school sometime later this evening? I want to look at the rooms and, if convenient, we can start setting them up for group discussion. Otherwise some of us will have to come in early tomorrow to get the rooms in order. It is very important in organising group discussion to arrange the rooms properly and in advance, so that there will be a minimum of confusion in getting discussion under way. We can mark the rooms A, B, C, etc., with chalk or placards. Who will bring chalk? Will someone volunteer to make some placards? In each room a sufficient number of chairs should be arranged in horseshoe shape, facing the blackboard (see Diagram) or better, around a large table or a rectangular group of tables. A small desk should be provided for the group reporter, near to that of the discussion leader. Two or three chairs should be put near the door for the use of observers, who will be popping in from time to time. (We observers will not say anything, so do not let our presence interrupt the group discussion.) The black-board should be erased, clean and there should be chalk, eraser and some paper for the reporter, but, as discussion leader, you need not worry too much about supplies. Go right ahead with the discussion even if supplies are lacking.

Controlling Discussion

Each participant will be given a list of discussion questions on a certain subject. All of the groups will discuss the same questions and the same subject — one which I am sure will interest all of you. I am not telling you what the subject will be, because we are here to learn how to conduct group discussion, not to learn about the

topic of the day. It would be just as well if you came tomorrow not knowing any more about the subject than the other participants. Your job is to keep the group discussion going smoothly, not to teach. In fact, a good discussion leader does not express his opinion on the questions being discussed. It is his job to control the discussion, to draw everyone into discussion and to restrain anyone who wants to dominate the group or to talk too much. In order to control discussion, you may want to make a list of your participants so that you can call them by name. Or you can just go around the circle from one person to the next, saying "Have you an opinion on this question?", "What have you to add?", "How would you put it in your own words?", "Has anyone a different opinion?", or "Who has something else to say?".

Here are some rules which will help you to control discussion:

- Be firm, tactful and understanding.
- To stimulate silent members:
  - the shy one – pass a direct, easy question;
  - the day-dreamer – redirect a question with a summary of the discussion so far;
  - the one with a chip on his shoulder – discover the cause of his grievance and put it to the group as a whole.
- To control over-talkative members:
  - the hostile one – seize upon a point he has made and put it to another member or to the group as a whole;
  - the "know-it-all" – do the same as for the hostile one;
  - the amiable wanderer – diplomatically bring him back to the point of discussion.

Do not express your own opinion. Do not try to teach. Just try to find out what the group thinks about the question and then, after sufficient discussion, summarize the group's opinion for the benefit of your reporter. If someone asks your opinion about a question, tell him that the director of studies instructed you not to give the answers. In any case, assure your group that their task is only to discuss and express their opinions. Tell them that experts with the correct answers will be there to answer their questions at the plenary session in the afternoon.

Now there is a way in which you can influence the discussion and also assist the learning process without appearing to do so. Suppose that someone proposes a wrong or stupid answer. Just move along and try to get some other opinion from the group, forgetting about the wrong answer, unless that person really insists. Suppose, then, that someone comes up with what sounds like a good answer. You may say to him: "Well, that is an interesting formulation. Will you kindly repeat that for us?". You may even write a few key words of the good answer on the blackboard, so that it gets full attention. In this way you have indirectly guided the discussion without the group realising it. We want them to feel that the answers recorded by your reporter are the findings of the group as a whole.

What if there is disagreement within the group as to which is the right answer? Now that is fine. That can lead to a lively discussion. Let them debate for a while, until they start repeating themselves. If they cannot convince one another, do not worry about it. Just say, at the right point, that discussion of this question has gone on long enough, and then suggest that the reporter write down a majority report and a minority report. You can ask the group to vote by a show of hands, but the reporter need not record the actual count. He should not attach anyone's name to any particular opinion. Just call it "majority report" and "minority report".

Do not worry if your group does not know the correct answer. The purpose of group discussion is not to find the correct answers. The purpose is "to soften the participants up", to prepare them so that they can learn from the experts who will appear for the afternoon session.

During the first half-hour, some of your participants may be frustrated. They may ask "What is this? We came here to learn something, not just to pool our ignorance." If this occurs, reassure them. The correct answers will come later. Tell them to please withhold judgment until the day is over, that the ILO expert has been using this method all over Ghana for the past four months and that workers everywhere seem to like it.

The questions have been designed to interest trade union officers. Some of the questions are difficult; no one may know the answers to some of them, but we have included them on purpose. The very fact that a question has been included will make the participants curious. They will think that it must be important, otherwise it would not have been included. After they have discussed it and reported on it, they will listen carefully to the expert, especially if there has been debate on a certain question. They will want to know which side the expert is going to uphold. Things that might have been forgotten had the expert delivered a lecture without group discussion, will now be remembered very well.

Do not let your group waste much time on any question for which the participants obviously do not know the answer. Do not let them make wild guesses. When that occurs, instruct your reporter to write down "We do not know". Do not be afraid to admit that your group does not know all of the answers.

Summing-up

Now have you any questions? I think that I have covered about all of the problems that might arise. Let me summarise just what you are expected to do. Will three or four of you volunteer to come in at 7.45 a.m. to help me set up the rooms, assuming that we cannot get that done this evening? Who will bring chalk and writing paper for the reporters? The rest of you should report to the school by 8 a.m. You may sit with the audience. After the opening ceremonies, I will take a few minutes to explain how we are going to run the seminar, and where to find rooms A, B, C, etc. I will then call for you who are here now to step up to the front. The Regional Secretary and I will have counted the number of participants actually present. We will divide this number by ten to determine the number of discussion groups. We will assign most of you as leaders of particular groups. The rest of you will be assigned to act as group reporters.

As soon as you are assigned, go to your room at once. Wait there for a few minutes until your participants arrive. We will give them little cards each with the letter of a room. We want to mix them all up so that the friends from a certain establishment or union will not be all together in one group. As soon as seven or eight of them have arrived, ask them to be seated in the chairs or on the benches, which will be arranged for group discussion. Ask them to put their name, the name of their union, and the position they hold in the union on a sheet of paper which you will circulate. You can use the list to call upon particular persons. While they are signing their names, you start the discussion. Read out question No. 1. Each of them will have the list of questions. Then read the question again for emphasis. You might write one or two key words on the board, but not the whole question. Ask them whether they understand the question and all of the words in it. Then let them discuss.

There are 17 questions on the list and you will have about three hours for discussion. That leaves about ten minutes for each question. Some of the questions are easy and will take little time. If the discussion seems fruitful, you may continue with any one question for about 20 minutes. But watch the clock. I will be going from one group to another, as will also Mr. X., who is the expert of the day. We will listen to the discussion. That will help us to answer the questions better in the afternoon session. Also, we want to improve the questions for the next time we use this topic. I will be watching to see whether your group is going too fast or too slow. If I point to my watch, it means you should move along faster. Or I may come up to you and whisper that your group is going too fast, so that you should leave more time to discuss each question. If your group should finish before 11.30, you may review some of the questions to get more complete answers. Just a "yes" or "no" is not sufficient, but each answer should be brief; a sentence or two may be enough.

After a question has been fully discussed, it is your job to summarize the answer and help the reporter to get it down in writing. After the group discussion is finished, you should sit down with your reporter and go over the answers. Be sure that they are clear and concise. Be sure that he has them arranged under 1(a), 1(b), etc., so that he can find them without hesitation. When the report has been edited, your job is done. We will call upon the reporters in the afternoon, but you may join the audience. You are free to take part in the general discussion. That will be your turn to raise questions with the expert or to express opinions, which you could not do during the group discussion.

Have you any questions? Will everyone read over page 2 of the paper entitled "How to Organise Group Discussion". Let us take five minutes to read it... Now have you any further questions?

Rehearsal

Let us take about five minutes more for a little practice in conducting group discussion. You are already sitting in a horseshoe shape. Will Mr. A. please come up here to act as discussion leader. Here is a list of questions for each of you. These are not the questions that we will use tomorrow. They are the ones which were used at Kumasi last month. Let us discuss one or two of them, just to show how it goes. Now, Mr. A., will you take over? I won't say anything for five or ten minutes. Then I will interrupt the discussion. We can then tell you how well you have handled the discussion. Remember, get everyone into the discussion and do not let anyone talk too much. This appears to be an aggressive group. Keep them under control.

After such a briefing, which lasted for one to one-and-a-half hours, the trainees were ready to serve as group discussion leaders on the following day. Each trainee was given a duplicated list of "Hints for Group Discussion Leaders" and some reading material about group discussion as a technique for adult education. Nothing was said about the subject matter to be discussed, the aim being to train discussion leaders, not teachers. In cumulative group discussion, the teacher appears as an "expert", answering questions after group discussion rather than lecturing beforehand.

Is the Labour Press "Educational"?

Much has been written lately – even in the columns of this publication – about the possibilities of using mass media in workers' education. The trend is evident in a great number of countries: unions and workers' education institutions are becoming increasingly aware of the benefits of mass media for educational purposes, even though education through these media touches larger audiences than their own membership and content and subject-matter must be presented differently for a wider, more differentiated public.

•

For well over one hundred years unions have educated their membership in the classroom, and only now are they trying out new ways of expanding their educational activities by turning to mass media. When one thinks of such media, radio and television immediately come to mind as the two most popular means of mass communication. This is natural enough, yet these techniques are comparatively new. Their educational potential is still far from being fully exploited, and this is particularly the case in the special field of workers' education. The impact of radio and television should not be neglected. But what about the oldest, yet still extremely important means of mass communication – the press?

Peterson, Jenson and Rivers[1] say about the press that it "can feed man the information he needs to formulate his own ideas; it can stimulate him by presenting the ideas of others. The press, in short, is one of the most pervasive and inexpensive of educators".

Although the beginnings of workers' education date back more than one hundred years and serious journalism can look back to a history of more than three centuries, it is astonishing to note that it was apparently not until one or two decades ago that some of the most important unions of North America and Europe began to worry about their rather distorted public relations image in the press. Only during the late fifties and the early sixties did they began to do something about it; by, for instance, feeding the press regularly with their own version of the facts and adopting more refined methods of treating the press as a partner in communicating with the public.

This change in attitude was largely brought about by a number of far-sighted men who recognised that inadequate or incomplete information about union matters could harm the aim pursued by trade unions and so hamper their work. In a lecture delivered at a conference on Union Public Relations at the University of Illinois on 28 January 1950, Ross Stagner illustrated the way is which

[1] Peterson, Jensen and Rivers: The Mass Media and Modern Society. Holt, Rinehart and Winston, Inc. New York 1965, 259 pp.

inadequate information can give a completely false impression, even when it is true, when he said: "Just listen to the following words and see what kind of a picture begins to get organised in your mind. Glass, Bottle, Alcohol, Noise, Men in white coats. Are you beginning to get a picture now? Suppose I add a cat. Does this change the picture? Now let me add a microscope and a dissecting set. What happens to your picture? I suspect that most of you had first built up a picture of a bar room, where the men in white coats were waiters and the alcohol was being used for drinking purposes. However, it becomes necessary to change the picture when new information about the microscope and the dissecting set is brought in; the whole thing changes over and becomes a scientific laboratory. The alcohol is used for preserving specimens. The men in white coats are doctors."

To inform accurately and completely is only one part of education. Perhaps more important in connection with workers' education is to convince. One should not forget that workers' education is almost exclusively aimed at adults, and that it therefore has to overcome many deeply rooted misconceptions and false interpretations in addition to disseminating factual knowledge.

Recognising this fact, unions began to organise news services on the level of the national federation or the international confederation, and these soon became a regular feature of their relations with communication media. These services can be found in almost all industrialised countries today, and they are constantly expanding the scope of the subjects covered. Steadily they improved in style and in most cases became reliable sources of information. However, publication of any item thus brought to the attention of editors depended on the latters' willingness to insert them in one of the daily or other periodicals which the public receives in the course of everyday life. If editors decided that certain types of information would not be of interest to the generality of their readers, such information did not appear. It is evident that any material which might serve the purpose of workers' education would receive rather scant attention from editors of the daily or weekly press, because it did not "make news". The news-oriented press, therefore, does not seem to be the right vehicle for labour-oriented educational matter.

At the same time, unions from the beginning have recognised the necessity of communicating regularly with their membership. They must report upon the union's activities, their successes or failures in collective bargaining and on other union affairs of direct interest to membership.

Depending on the unions' size, an almost incredible number of publications shot up, ranging from simple mimeographed newsletters, written in stilted language and often secretly produced after working hours on the employers' duplicating machines, to highly sophisticated journals featuring pretty cover girls and carrying union slogans, printed in magazine-type multicoloured format. Recent surveys on the production of union periodicals conducted in the United States and the Federal Republic of Germany showed fabulous figures: the 1964 Ayer and Son's directory of periodicals listed 254 labour publications in the United States; 180 among them reported a total circulation of 9,800,000 (estimates of the total labour press coverage in the United States go as far as 30 million a month). The 1970 list of publications of the German Confederation of Trade Unions (DGB) contains forty-four periodicals with a total circulation of well over 6 million, to which about as many copies should be counted which are published by regional and local organisations as well as by unions not affiliated to the DGB.

A closer look at these impressive figures reveals that in most of these publications – with a few exceptions – about one-third of the space is taken up by reports on collective bargaining, one-third on internal union affairs such as elections, announcements of meetings, etc. Roughly 15 per cent is devoted to political action and only 5 per cent is reserved for educational subjects such as information on economic matters, population and the work force. The rest is filled with organisational activities such as unionisation of the unorganised work force and other questions. Among

vox populi

the items of no direct union concern published in these periodicals the most common are fraternal intelligence (social notes about members), news of the trade, technical articles, public charity and social causes, poetry, fiction and general-interest cartoons and photographs. There is also advertising matter.

An ILO-sponsored workshop in Geneva in 1961 analysed publications of the labour press with regard to their appeal to the reader, the attractiveness of the published copy, make-up and print. Labour journalists from general parts of the world exchanged information about the labour press in their respective countries, in order to get new ideas from which their own publications might be made more attractive.

Many new union journals have appeared in recent years. Some of the most outstanding are perhaps *Hallo* and *Solidarität*, both edited and printed by the Austrian Trade Union Federation in Vienna. Competing with the public press and with the advent of colour television, both publications are printed in colour, and contain articles of high quality, sometimes artistically illustrated. Among the topics treated in these publications are discussions of some of the burning issues of day-to-day life. Such publications show that the unions are now beginning to realise the educational value of a well-produced press. Attractively presented, they are in fact becoming increasingly valuable instruments of workers' education.

It took a long time for workers' educators and journalists to realise that their vocations have many points in common: they are required to present factual knowledge so as to render it digestible for the learners' – or readers' – minds. This is probably the reason why many great educators have also been great writers – Pestalozzi is just one example. On the other hand journalists, having the gift or talent of clear expression, did not always realise that this is also a prerequisite of good teaching.

In view of this affinity one may ask whether the labour press may not be expected to perform a greater educational task, and if so, whether it will live up to this expectation.

Before considering this question, the following factors should be borne in mind:

First of all, the labour press cannot be compared with the general public press, as it does not have access to the resources which are generally available to other periodicals or newspapers. The complex organisation of a general interest daily newspaper cannot be achieved even in the most efficient editorial office of a labour journal. While the *New York Times* is written by a staff of 934 editors, correspondents and reporters, a union paper is more likely to be produced by one man who has to do everything: writing, editing, correspondence, reporting, photographic coverage, preparing the dummy for the printer and reading the proofs. In doing all this he will hardly find time to produce good educational copy which is not only well written but is laid out according to pedagogically sound principles so that readers will not find it difficult to assimilate.

Second, many labour journalists never "learned their job" in a professional way. They came into their profession with a good deal of zeal, felt that they had to be aggressive and paid little attention to the more subtle and at the same time more objective techniques by which more effective results can generally be achieved. Recently, some unions have recognised the need for training labour journalists, and are sponsoring seminars and courses by which editors of labour periodicals may learn simple techniques, such as how to write a press release, how to organise copy for publication and other tricks of the trade.

Third, the originally rather limited field of interest of the labour press is widening only at a slow pace. New fields of union action contribute to this process as they come along: participation in planning demands of union members a better understanding of basic economics, and union periodicals help to provide the factual material and elements for such understanding. This in itself is already an educational contribution – but the average reader would probably prefer to go to the public library where more comprehensive material would be at hand than can be conveyed in piecemeal form by even the bulkiest labour journal.

Fourth, some labour journals have therefore made it a practice to join forces with other sources of knowledge by giving information about these to their readers. They give advice on which books to read, what records to buy, which television or radio programme to tune in to and on many other matters.

Fifth, some – unfortunately only too few – labour periodicals have recognised the fact that their own physical image does not compare with that of the professional press: layout, photographs, illustrations and printing are not attractive enough to invite extensive reading. UAW's *Solidarity* is a good example of how a union magazine, by employing a gifted photographer, may improve its image and become a publication whose arrival is eagerly awaited by the subscriber every month.

Other problems which the editor of a labour journal may have to cope with may include the receipt of contributions written by inexperienced colleagues who suddenly feel an urge to plunge into journalism; unusable photographs which he cannot publish and which he often loses in piles of similar material and has to search for when the disappointed contributor asks for their return, plus administrative problems of all kinds – and for all this perhaps the assistance of just one overworked faithful secretary. Over the weekend the editor must attend conferences and meetings. How can he still find time to think about his paper's contributions towards the education of his union's membership, let alone write them?

Difficulties of that nature are abundant. However, there is increasing evidence that unions are paying more attention to these questions and are giving fresh thought to ways of improving educational facilities for workers. Labour journals are still the most important and often the only means of permanent communication between unions and their membership. They could be more than just this link; they could become major instruments of workers' education.

One way by which some progress could perhaps be achieved would be for workers' educators to consult their colleagues in their unions' editorial offices, to search for the best ways of producing material for publication in the labour press and, further, once it was published, how it could be exploited by perhaps using the standing type and blocks to produce printed material for subsequent courses. This might relieve the editor of some of his writing chores and at the same time ease the usually strained educational budget of a union. A few examples of this kind of collaboration in the recent past resulted in handsome booklets which appeared in the United States and which were produced at no more than the cost of paper and machine time.

Educational bodies outside the union, such as universities, could be tapped to produce material for publication in the labour press and the list of topics which would be of educational value to workers in our world today becomes longer as technology develops. Workers' education in the 1970's is no longer a relatively simple matter. It has gained in momentum and in complexity. Every means possible must be used to cope with its increased responsibilities. The labour press represents one way, and a very important way, of helping workers better to understand the changing environment of work and life. ■

Curt Fernau

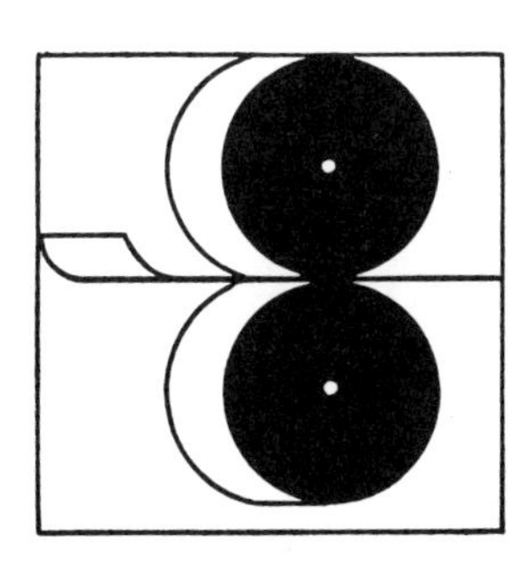

The reading club: movies without pictures

André GRANOUILLAC
Director of Economic and
Social Studies
Confédération Force Ouvrière,
France

For those who deal with training, the search for new methods is a constant preoccupation. The development of audio-visual means (tape recorders, flannelboards, slide projectors, etc.) has made a great contribution toward opening the eyes of those who have believed for a long time that all that was necessary to be an educator was to talk down to a class from the heights of a platform. Traditional methods have lost their supremacy for the teaching of children, and even more so for the teaching of adults who have learned from their own experience that training is first and foremost a matter of interchange and dialogue.

Sometimes the search for new methods may appear to be a useless luxury, a sort of gadget which appeals to trainers who primarily want novelty for novelty's sake. Some experiments, which make use of the most modern materials of pedagogical research are of such a nature, and it is impossible to exaggerate how important it is to use them with reservation. In contrast, other experiments which have been fully studied and checked and which deserve a wide reputation are found to be poorly understood and little used. This is true of the "reading club", *which we thought it would be interesting to introduce to the readers of the "Bulletin".*

Movies without Pictures

The trainees have deserted the usual room used for lectures and group work. Now they are meeting in the library after dinner. They are not sitting at neatly arranged tables, but in a semi-circle of armchairs. The lights are dim. The animator is seated behind a little table in the corner with a desk lamp. A closed book is in front of him.

When everybody is quiet, the animator simply announces the title of the book and the name of the author, *325,000 Francs, by Roger Vailland*[1], and he starts to read.

The bicycle race of Bionnas is contested every year on the first Sunday of May by the best amateur cyclists in six French Departments: Ain, Rhône, Isère, Jura, and the two Savoies. It is a stiff test of endurance. The riders have to pedal over the pass of the Croix Rousse three times at an altitude of 1,250 metres.

A few minutes later, the unlucky hero of this story makes his appearance – Bernard Busard, who abandons cycling to take a factory job, hoping to earn enough money to win his way through to love and liberty.

The reading continues for about an hour, never more, sometimes less, and during that hour the listeners live through the adventures of the hero of the story. Those who watch the animator carefully will notice that he is not reading the whole book consecutively, that sometimes he skips over a dozen pages, that on one page he may read ten lines, and only five or six on the next page. Nevertheless, they find that everything holds together logically, as in a film.

The animator comes to the end of the book. He reads the last lines: *Busard will now earn 190 francs*[2] *an hour. The wave of anger that resulted from his mutilation had set off a general strike which won a further 10 franc raise. Thus he gets a workers' disability pension;* then the animator closes the book.

Generally, the group remains silent, as people are silent after having listened to Mozart, and do not immediately re-adapt to the sounds of daily life. Then feet move, chairs are pushed back, someone coughs or lights a cigarette. Then the animator says simply, *I have just read you a montage based on the text of this novel. In this montage, what pictures stand out most strongly in your memory? Which ones do you remember the best?* Then everybody starts talking at once, and little by little, out of the disorder, the whole story is reconstructed within a few minutes.

The animator quickly learns what has been most striking, by the spontaneous reactions of the group when these mental pictures are evoked. Sometimes those elements which initially seem most dramatic are scarcely referred to, whereas tiny and insignificant facts may come out with great force and detail.

Now begins the active part of the reading club. The animator guides a discussion which has as its purpose to lead the participants step by step:

- to reconstruct the sequence of the story;
- to understand the situation, and the personality of the characters and their relationships;
- to probe for the meaning of the work;
- to compare and contrast it to daily life;
- to explain the why and the how of the situation;
- to round out the presentation of the work and the author;
- to reach decisions leading to action.

If the discussion is to be worth while, it must have good leadership. The animator should not rush past the stages for any reason whatsoever, or let others rush past them. For example, in the first phase of evoking the images, he should not let people who know more than the others talk about the author or set forth their views on the work as a whole. By using a progressive development of questions with a view to a real "mental training" the animator should engage each of his listeners into an active interplay.

• Thus, briefly reconstructing the development of the story is, in itself, an excellent exercise in expression. Many people who are blocked when they have to talk about themselves, or about abstract subjects, become excellent story-tellers, sensitive to detail and to logic, when they deal with subjects outside themselves.

• When the animator asks for examples from personal experience, so that the group may judge the distance between fiction and fact, the participants are sometimes surprised to realise what a wealth of experience each one has, and how worth while it is to listen to the old-timers and to those who have been lucky enough to travel abroad.

• When, finally, he presents the author of the novel, when he refers to other books and to the cinema, and makes comparisons with films on

[1] *This of course represents but an example taken by chance from a novel of Contemporary French Literature.*

[2] *Old francs.*

the same subject, he helps each one to get a better insight into outside sources of information – books, moving pictures, newspapers, television.

This shows how important the role of the animator is, and it also shows, above all, how carefully basic materials should be arranged. These two points are worth further development.

One Novel – Seven Montages

There are many good novels (and if there isn't one which is suitable to your purpose in your own language, it is always possible to turn to translations). However, the choice of a novel for a reading club is not an easy matter.

- First of all, a choice of a work which is easy to read aloud. Frequently you find excellent novels, written with long and complicated sentences and unusual vocabulary, so that it is impossible to read them aloud. However fine they may be, they cannot be used for a reading club.

- It must also be possible to make reading selections from the book which is chosen, so that one or more characters can be brought out clearly in the framework of a pre-selected plot.

- The story that is told must not be too alien from the lives of the group. For example, the story shouldn't recount the sentimental complications of the idle rich on the Côte d'Azur or in California, since militants in workers' associations are going to be indifferent to this type of problem.

To make a successful sequence from a novel which has been chosen in this way, it is necessary to know the book thoroughly, to have read and re-read it several times. When you feel that there is something to be gotten out of a book, the only method is that of trial and error. Cheap editions (usually pocket books) make it possible to work out several montages at little cost since frequently entire paragraphs have to be struck out, and all the pages which are to be skipped over should be stapled together. Sometimes a few words have to be written in to link together the material.

There are but few rules that will provide guidance here: it is through experience that each animator develops his own. Although, in France, mention should be made of the outstanding role in this work played by the leaders of the "People and Culture" association; it should also be made clear that any trained animator acquainted with both literature and the people with whom he works can develop his own experimental montages. It is, moreover, worth noting that, as each reading follows its predecessor, you are led to make changes in the script sequences, sometimes as to details, sometimes even more radically. Speaking of his own experience, this writer is at work on his seventh montage of *"325,000 Francs"* by Roger Vailland, and has available one montage drawn from this text which is specifically oriented around trade union problems, another montage which focuses on matters of safety at work, a third based on the character of a peasant who becomes an industrial worker, a fourth on the part played by women in matters of professional ambition, etc. This, in passing, indicates how rich this novel is, though few had heard of it before the French television made an adaptation of it. What an additional source of satisfaction it is for an animator to discover novels of this sort!

Dominant Idea and Adaptability

Whether the animator-reader himself constructs the montage or whether he makes use of material developed by others, his success depends on the way in which the reading club evolves, and the extent to which it leads to further activity.

The animator should be guided by two concerns:

- He should have one basic training idea uppermost in his mind: he may wish to develop *skills in self-expression* among his trainees, he may wish to train them in the *analytical and experimental observation* of the groups among whom they live; or he may want to *draw their attention to educational sources and self-training.*

In the first case, he will primarily try to get people to talk, to tell their story. His questions and his suggestions will facilitate expression by all the participants.

Statistics on books and reading in France show that 2,500 publishers issue about 250 million copies of their books each year, which are sold through some 30,000 retail outlets. But the figures also indicate that 75 per cent of the books published are read by only 15 per cent of the French population. And what is more, 58 per cent of the French never read a book.

In the second case, he will use his questions to prompt as objective an analysis as possible of the most interesting experiences of the members of the group, and out of this, working with the group, he will draw the materials for a programme of inquiry or for a questionnaire.

In the final case, he will encourage people to read the whole work (giving practical references for buying or borrowing it from a library) and will build up a file based on a bibliography of works by the same author, or on the same subject and including a reproduction of criticisms or press notices.

Obviously, this is only a dominant idea, and a given animator who has chosen to prompt his trainees to read the book may also take advantage of the contribution of a participant so as to bring the listeners to a fuller knowledge of the milieu in which they live by making a more objective analysis of it.

• The second concern of the animator has to do with his degree of adaptability. If the group doesn't go along with his initial strategy, he must change it. It might happen that a montage of texts intended to illustrate the problems of safety on the job gradually veers around, under the influence of the group discussion, toward consideration of questions of speed-up and the part played by shop stewards. If the listeners have a strong motivation for this centre of interest, the animator must go along with his group, even though, later on, he may return to his initial interest, in a round-about way. Obviously a distinction should be made between casual discussion that drifts off the subject due to isolated disrupters (and there are many who have to be swung back into line) and the different orientations, deeply felt by virtually all the group. The important thing for the animator is to follow the general group feeling in his training action, always with the possibility of using detours.

An Effective Method

It is up to every training leader to develop and maintain a whole set of skills if he is to animate a reading club. Even if he does not work out the montage himself – and this is perfectly possible – the animator must bear in mind a certain number of general rules:

- *the reading* must be fluent (which implies prior rehearsals); it must be neither too flat nor too

theatrical, and it should maintain a good speed which everybody can follow;

- *the discussion* should be definitely guided as to its general direction, but it should be very flexible for the development of each phase; questions providing orientation should be prepared in advance;

- the animator's *files* should be well supplied with press clippings, book reviews, a biography of the author, a bibliography on the subject, etc., and it should also make room for related elements: reports on research, statistics, photos, newspaper clippings, etc.;

- it should be a matter of concern for the animator to *check the results:* if he initiates an inquiry, he should follow up on the results himself; if he has assigned others to read books, he should ask for reports about them, etc.

●

If these conditions are met, the reading club quickly proves to be one of the most effective methods of adult training. With little cost (and this is frequently important) it opens the door to an appreciation of the value of books for our culture, broad exchanges of real-life experiences, interesting contributions in the field of expression, analysis of the environment and of documentation.

When it is seen as part of the over all subject of the self-development of the personality, the reading club is one of the means most adapted to what might be called "mental training".

Labour Education's Best Friend:

The tape recorder

The tape recorder is a teaching aid whose importance, for the purposes of labour education, must be underlined. Though its relatively high cost is often an obstacle to its general use, the services it can render deserve the attention of the workers' educationist.

This article is not intended to list all the possible uses of the tape recorder in programmes of workers' education or to constitute a full technical manual for the use of this machine. It will merely outline three essential uses workers' education can assign to the tape recorder and offer a few words of advice with a view to facilitating its purchase and utilisation.

In the first place, when travelling, the instructor possessing a tape recorder will have all facilities for recording courses which are given centrally or nationally and whose importance and interest justify a wider diffusion. The same also applies to reports, speeches or statements by national leaders, whose content registers more effectively by being heard rather than by a mere printed copy. At a study course, an interview recorded with a trade union, academic or other personality on a problem related to the subjects under study can provide a moment of relaxation or even an opportunity for discussion which is far from being a waste of time. It goes without saying that any radio or television broadcast, lecture, group discussion or simple record can be registered on magnetic tape and kept, and the tape can later be rubbed out and used again for a new recording. The magnetic recording has the great advantage that it can be interrupted, cut, re-edited; it is thus an ideal instrument for analysing a discussion or criticising a report or speech.

* * *

According to Plutarch, Demosthenes corrected his faults in elocution by placing a number of small pebbles in his mouth when addressing the ocean waves. The tape recorder today provides a less irksome method. The " lesson " it can give in public speaking points to another interesting use for this machine in labour education.

Public speaking is one of the normal functions of trade union officials, and many senior and experienced activists will admit that this is an exercise which necessitates a long and arduous apprenticeship. Eloquence, long since cast aside, can be a natural gift but the art of presenting a subject of study in a clear and logical manner goes far beyond mere eloquence and remains a basic quality to be acquired by the educationist. In this connection, the tape recorder can render valuable service. The pupil can be called upon to make an exposé to be recorded and presented to the study group. The ensuing group criticism will provide an appreciable element of progress. Apart from this, when exposés made personally by the pupils are recorded on the tape recorder, this procedure ensures a revival of interest on the pupil's part as well as a remarkable improvement in their method of expression. Realising this, the Italian Metal Workers' Union, for example, has made it a rule to record all group discussions and to let the pupils listen to these recordings so as to encourage them to develop the spirit of self-criticism with regard to their own statements.

* * *

Finally, with the help of the tape recorder, the workers' educationist can record commentaries on films, and is thus spared the trouble of repeating the commentary each time the same film is shown.

* * *

These three essential uses give some idea of the role which the tape recorder can play in workers' education. The few technical tips which follow have been taken from the British Magazine OVAC, published in London by the Oversea Visual Aids Centre, and have been reproduced by kind permission of the editors. They will obviously not answer every question which may be raised by the purchaser or user of a tape recorder, but they will provide the novice with some essential basic elements which will facilitate his choice of machine and help him to get acquainted with its operation and maintenance.

Robert Falaize

To build up a nation, every individual, as a member of society, must strive to develop his intellectual capacities and raise his standard of living.

(Léopold Senghor)

Choice, upkeep and use of the tape recorder

Intelligibility or high fidelity?

What degree of so-called *High Fidelity* do you want? This poses another question—*what is high fidelity?* Nothing has created so much argument in the technical world as this term. Theoretically we should aim at being able to record and play back as accurately as possible the original sounds, and broadly speaking this may be termed *high fidelity*. There are many occasions however where a high degree of accuracy is not required, the main requirement being intelligibility. If you want a machine mainly for recording speech then perhaps a cheaper machine may meet your requirements. Generally speaking, the higher the fidelity you want the higher the cost. An indication of how good a recorder is regarding fidelity can be assessed by looking at the *Frequency Response* quoted in the manufacturers' literature. It is not sufficient for the manufacturer to quote frequency response figures unless he also quotes the decibel (bB) variation. A good figure is around ± 2dB.

Battery or mains operation?

This depends upon whether you have mains electricity available or if you require complete mobility. Mains electricity machines can be operated from car batteries provided a suitable converter is used. Unfortunately the type of converter required is expensive. Most battery-operated tape-recorders of the dry or torch battery type can be operated from mains electricity with a suitable converter. The main drawback with most battery-operated machines is the small spool size. This can be compensated by using thinner tapes, such as long play, double play or triple play tapes.

Two track or four track?

How many people with a four track machine really use all four tracks? Probably very few. This is mainly due to the difficulty they experience in finding the required track on the tape quickly. The question of signal to noise ratio, seen in most specifications as SIG/NOISE RATIO requires consideration when discussing two or four track recorders. The *signal* is the material you wish to record (speech or music). Obviously the perfect recording is that which has no noise and only signal. In practice we never get this. The best we can hope for is as wide a ratio as possible between the signal and the noise. A good figure for this is around 50dB. Generally speaking the signal to noise ratio is better and a wider frequency response may be found in a two track machine.

Tape speeds

A well-made machine with a speed of 3 3/4" per second will be found suitable for most work.

Power output

This is quoted by manufacturers in " Watts ". As a very rough guide 3 watts output could be considered sufficient for a group of about 40 people, but there are other factors such as the type of room you are in, and its furniture and fittings, or whether you are playing-back indoors or outdoors.

Revolution counter or indicator

Some models offer this facility which helps you to find a certain place on the tape.

Pause control

This device enables you to stop the tape momentarily without switching the machine to stop, thus avoiding " clicks " in recording.

Attention !

Few recorders, however impressive their specifications and performance, can be expected to give trouble-free use indefinitely especially under difficult climatic conditions. Before making a final decision to buy a particular model, *find out what servicing facilities are available in the country where you are going to use it*. This is a precaution sometimes overlooked with melancholy consequences.

Care of Tape Recorder

Recording head

The actual recording gap on this electro magnet is very narrow and you will have a serious loss of high frequencies if it is allowed to get dirty. Clean with a soft cloth dipped in carbon-tetrachloride or methylated spirits. When switching to or from " record", have the volume control as low as possible. Never touch the recording head with anything metallic.

Erase head

If allowed to get dirty, the erase head may not completely remove your previous recording and your new recording will be spoiled. Clean carefully with CTC.

Tape spools

If these are bent or out of alignment they may catch on the tape and cause wow or flutter. If plastic spools are badly bent they can be immersed in very hot water and pressed back into shape.

Transistors

Transistors do not like high temperatures. Do not keep any transistorised recorder in a closed car exposed to the hot sun. Never use a transistorised recorder when the temperature is over 100° F.

Batteries

Use sealed leak-proof batteries if possible. They are more likely to be fresh and will not damage the recorder through corrosion when exhausted. Use fresh batteries for any special recording.

Recording techniques

Acoustics

Avoid reflecting surfaces which give a boomy bathroom effect. The lack of soft furnishings leads to reverberations. Cover plain walls and floors with curtains, carpets or cushions to get a more " dead " effect. Have a soft cloth on the table which holds the microphone.

Microphone position

- Keep the microphone away from the recorder (not on the same table) otherwise it will pick up the sound of the motor.
- Speak about one foot from the microphone. Talk past or over the microphone.
- In an interview, make sure that you balance the voices and have the same recording level.
- Do not hold the microphone in your hand. Do not jog the table on which the microphone is standing.
- Be continually on the alert for unwanted sounds. Get close to the sound to be recorded in order to cut down the ratio of interference or wait for a period of comparative quiet.
- Avoid the rustle of notes and papers near the microphone.
- When recording out of doors, guard against wind currents by tying across the face of your microphone one thickness of handkerchief.

Controls

Speeds. 3 3/4 ips for quality. 1 7/8 ips for speech only, when a wide range of tones is not required.

Start/Stop. Let the machine gather speed before starting to record.

Volume. To steer a middle course between overmodulation and under-recording you need to keep a constant watch on the recording indicator. Overmodulation leads to distortion and under-recording means that the volume has to be turned up on playback thus increasing the background hiss and hum.

Make several trial recordings to check acoustics, mike position, controls, speakers, etc.

Microphone methods

- Get people to speak slowly, particularly at the beginning when listeners are getting used to their voices.
- If possible, work from notes and not from a full written script. It is far more difficult to sound natural and interesting when reading a prepared manuscript.
- In interviews, identify the speaker or lead him to identify himself.
- Try to get the person interviewed to do most of the talking.
- Plan your questions and discuss the general subject with the interviewee beforehand. Then conduct your interview before the microphone with just a list of questions.
- *And if in doubt about your recording, do it twice.*

The Rules of the Game

Why should sport, which thrills the crowds, not serve labour education purposes? Such was the line of thought of this trade union instructor—a football referee of unquestionable authority—who was wont to quote practices observed in football, rugby or boxing, to reinforce his arguments when lecturing to his audience. "Let us take the case of a football match", he would say, " and let us imagine that one of the teams knew neither the rules of the game nor had undergone any preliminary training. Imagine the confusion! And what a run of penalties! What would the referee do in such a case: penalise those eager but ill-equipped players or, to avert a calamitous defeat, suggest that they withdraw to the sports pavilion and report for subsequent training?" Is it not, moreover, only just and fair that all competitors enjoy the same training privileges and facilities? The lively comparisons between professional and amateur sport—with the many parallels to be drawn in workers' education—more than held the attention of his audience.

Then, with his inherent and keen sportsman attitude, this dynamic pedagogue would turn from football to boxing. He would conjure up a picture of a contest between two opponents, one of whom wore no gloves. The would-be pugilist could doubtless deal his adversary many a hard blow, but would he not run the risk of broken bones? Thus modern society, he would add, demands equal opportunities for all; it will no longer tolerate fighting with bare hands, a form of contest that has caused too much blood to flow in the past. In the same way, education of the workers, just as that of the employers and public authorities, assumes the obligation to transform a merciless and frequently endless struggle into a loyal debate between partners of equal standing, leading to a mutually acceptable solution.

To be familiar with the rules of the game, to be capable of applying them or enforcing their application, if need be to respect and obey the referee's decision—such is the law of sport, and that of society should be no different. Moreover, our referee-instructor always took pains to add that the rules of the game—if they have to be studied—are always open to modification. *R.F.*

A witness to be believed

The Tape-Recorder and its Use for Labour Education Courses in Algeria

The article in *Labour Education* No. 2 on the tape-recorder as an aid to workers' education outlined three primary uses, stressing in particular that " the magnetic recording has the great advantage that it can be interrupted, cut, re-edited ; it is thus an ideal instrument for analysing a discussion or criticising a report or speech ".

In this connection the experiment carried out by ILO expert Mr. Marius Apostolo, while on mission in Algeria from 22 October 1964 to 10 March 1965, is worth describing in some detail.

•

Preparing a Lecture

From 16 to 28 November 1964 the General Union of Algerian Workers (UGTA) organised a national course for workers' educators at the Drarini Mohamed Trade Union College near Algiers. Each of the 17 regional trade union centres was invited to select for participation in the course two of its most active officials who showed promise as potential educators. The National Workers' Education Service had stressed the need to choose as far as possible candidates who had already participated at the regional level in a basic training course in the general principles of trade unionism.

Twenty-six workers were accepted for the course.

The syllabus consisted on the one hand of lectures on trade unionism and political economy and on the other hand of a series of lecture-and-discussion sessions (scope and content of workers' education; how to prepare and give a lecture; how to lead and stimulate discussion; methods and techniques of workers' education; study programme and schedule), as well as an exposé on the organisational problems encountered in workers' education.

The aims of the National Education Service and of the ILO expert were to raise the general educational standard of prospective educators, impart to them the rudiments of teaching and give them practical guidance in organising educational activities in their local or regional union.

It was obviously not enough simply to give the students theoretical training as to how they should set about preparing and giving a lecture, or leading and stimulating discussion. They had to be given a chance to put what they had learned into practice while still at the College, as well as to analyse and assess as a group the results of their first efforts.

This explains why a great deal of time was devoted to practical activities.

The main theme of the course was " The Role and Structure of the UGTA "; this theme was chosen precisely because of the difficulty seemingly met by most of the students in dealing with such a subject.

After a talk by the expert on how to prepare and give a lecture, the students were split up into three working groups of more or less identical experience.

The trainee educators had first of all to prepare a lecture on the main theme of the course and then to deliver their lecture to the rest of their fellow students.

In view of the limited time available each group was made responsible for a specific part of the lecture. Thus the first group had to prepare the introduction to the theme together with the first part of the lecture dealing with the Union's internal and external activities and interests. The second group had to submit the intermediate part relating to the structure and framework of the Union, while the third considered the duties and responsibilities of branch officials and, in addition, established the conclusions.

The training was carried out in three stages:

(1) *individual* study of documentation supplied by the course organisers and planning of the study group lecture assignment;
(2) *group* discussion within each group, led by an animator, to study and consider the principal suggestions;
(3) *personal* drafting of the part of the lecture that had been assigned to each group.

The students had been warned in advance that a trainee educator from each group would be selected by the course organisers to undertake the presentation of his group's lecture assignment to the student body as a whole. All the participants were then required to evaluate the quality of individual lectures, based on three main criteria: outline of the lecture assignments, structure, and sequence of ideas; subject matter; value of the teaching method used.

•

It was at this point that the tape recorder came into play as an extremely valuable aid to workers' education.

It can indeed be asserted that the tape recorder was one of the factors mainly responsible for the successful results achieved at the end of the course.

The method adopted was as follows:

The student lecturer appointed from the first group had to stand in front of the microphone of the tape recorder, facing his fellow students. His presentation of the first part of the lecture was recorded. During this time the other students had to jot down their observations on the basis of the three criteria listed above.

At the end of the talk—which should not exceed 15 to 20 minutes—the tape was played back, thus enabling the students to add to their notes and the speaker to assess his own performance.

A general discussion followed under the leadership of one of the course organisers or of the ILO expert.

Several times it was necessary to " replay " part of the tape to illustrate comments made about the subject matter of the talk or about its value from a teaching point of view.

The same method was used for each lecture assignment undertaken by the trainee educator selected from the three individual groups.

It then fell to the ILO expert to draw conclusions from the experiment as a whole.

•

Leading and Stimulating Discussion

In this context the tape recorder demonstrated another of its uses during the training course.

Following an analytical talk on " How to lead and stimulate discussion ", the three selected group educators had to lead a general discussion on their own lecture assignment prepared a few days previously.

Each trainee educator had studied in advance several standard questions which were submitted for group consideration and subsequently discussed in plenary session. One educator was chosen to lead the discussion.

Their boon companion, the tape recorder, once again had its part to play. A living and impartial witness, it highlighted both the successes and the shortcomings of the task performed.

At each stage of this training project, the trainee educators thus had an opportunity to evaluate more thoroughly the techniques of leading and stimulating discussion, the points raised in general debate, and the animator's summing up. This was rendered all the easier by the fact that the tape recorder could reproduce as desired any part of the recorded proceedings.

In addition, the ILO expert and the UGTA course organisers themselves learned a great deal from the experiment.

An Implacable Witness

Broadly speaking, the trainees were delighted that the tape recorder had been used. Not only did they have a chance to serve a practical apprenticeship in their role as educators, but the use of this tool had afforded live recordings from which the trainees could judge their individual performance, discern personal shortcomings, and pinpoint various features calling for improvement on their part.

Women trainee educators attended a similar course shortly afterwards and found it an equally satisfactory experience. Even more use was made of the tape recorder than during the preceding course for men trainees.

The syllabus included a practical exercise on how to plan and organise a trade union branch meeting.

The students appointed a chairwoman for the meeting, a reporter and a clerk.

After preparatory group work the project opened with a talk by the chairwoman, followed by the reporter's introduction of her subject: "Why promote workers' education for women workers?" While the tape recorder lent an attentive ear, a broad discussion followed under the lead of the chairwoman.

At the end of the meeting the trainees were set the task of evaluating their work, aided by the magnetic tape. The chairwoman, for instance, who had taken pains during the debate to minimise pointless discussion, realised that she herself had perhaps conducted the proceedings with praiseworthy but somewhat exaggerated authority.

At the close of the course the magnetic tape was again used to record popular music broadcast on the national radio network, a recording which subsequently provided background music for a social gathering. That same evening the machine recorded a song composed by a trainee educator, when use of the tape recorder again met with unanimous approval.

All things considered, the ILO expert, the UGTA organisers and the trainees had reason to congratulate themselves on having made use of such a valuable educational aid.

●

Certainly the tape recorder should not be looked upon as a panacea ; valuable as it is, it cannot be more than an aid. It is likewise important to regulate its use according to circumstances—as should be done, incidentally, with all audio-visual aids.

Subject to these reservations, the tape recorder occupies a place of honour among practical aids, as it enables the worker to discover for himself his own personality and to develop his capabilities.

Montaigne counselled the educator to work " within the intellectual capacity of the person in his charge ... giving him free play to taste, to choose and to discern things for himself, sometimes pointing out to him the way, sometimes letting him discover it for himself ".

Is this not precisely the kind of perspective which the tape recorder opens out to workers' educators?

THE TAPE RECORDER ...

... THE ZEALOUS TRAINEE AND AN " ELOQUENT " REWARD

What is the flannelboard?

This was precisely the question which I asked myself when—some twelve years ago—I was invited to attend a lecture about civic rights and responsibilities in the Federal Republic of Germany. There, many activities were going on at that time in the field of adult education. In lecture groups and discussion clubs formed by various bodies audio-visual aids were extensively applied.

•

Not that adult education was something new in this country, but the way one went about it, the approach—as it was called—differed in many respects from that to which one had been accustomed up till then. There was, of course, the lecture accompanied by films and filmstrips, which always presented some special attraction. But there was something else, hitherto unknown, which has since become the common property of many a lecturer: a whole range of audio-visual aids other than classic films and filmstrips.

And in the course of that one evening when a lecturer from an adult education centre talked about the structure of Government in a democracy, the programme indicated a flannelboard that he would use. What was this? I had never seen one before, never even heard about it.

When the speaker began to explain how Government worked and how voters could influence its policy, the audience was listening more or less listlessly. They seemed to know all about it. But when, after some five or ten minutes, the speaker turned towards the blackboard in the corner, holding some funny looking symbols in his hand which seemed to be cut from cardboard, everybody was intrigued to know how these " paper heroes ", as the lecturer called them, adhered to the board and showed no signs of falling off. The interest among the group grew immensely. Why was this?

Effect of the Flannelboard Technique

It is difficult to answer this question in precise terms. In the first place, there seemed to be the effect of something new. The different symbols used by the speaker, prepared by him and obviously not the work of an experienced draftsman, helped to illustrate his talk. In using the prefabricated symbols, he constantly faced the audience and never lost contact for a moment. Nor did he lose any time as he would have done, had he used the blackboard on which to draw the same figures. Also, drawing them on the blackboard would have meant that the speaker was obliged to turn his back to the group for quite some time, during which the audience might conceivably have dozed off for a few seconds.

The room always remained lit, which would not have been the case had he used slides for example. In fact, the lecture went on so smoothly and fast, that people had no chance to let their thoughts stray from the topic.

The speaker, in his treatment of the rather serious and dry subject, nevertheless succeeded at the same time in bringing out the human side: his drawings were of the caricature type, even with some similarity to living and well-known politicians. The symbols he used were simple, almost too easy to understand. They left no room for false interpretation. This helped tremendously to illustrate the complexities of Government machinery.

As the lecturer added one symbol after another to his board, they all began to shape up and form a complete chart showing at a glance the topic as a whole. And when post-lecture discussion started, he was able to adjust the set-up of his " visuals " according to each question, removing or adding elements as necessary. He had prepared his speech so well, that he had even anticipated some questions posed by the group, for which he had new " paper heroes " in readiness so as to reinforce his explanations.

This success was not because he had the natural gift of being a good orator—he was not. On the contrary: as he had repeatedly spoken on the same topic, he was familiar with all its aspects. He had probably improved some of his symbols, had tested them to see whether they got the intended message across. But time and time again the old game of how to capture his listeners seemed to fascinate him. He did not let the devil out of his box until the audience had settled and had tacitly begun to convey the impression that this speaker would be like many others—more or less boring. And it was precisely at this moment that he began his little show. This speaker chose the so-called moment of truth, and the effect was only too obvious: he shocked the group gently, at the moment when some of them—after a long day's work—were just thinking about taking a short cat-nap with eyes open.

How and When to Use the Flannelboard

Here we enter a field which in recent years has become a speciality of its own and to which much thought has been given: group therapy.

A flannelboard demonstration, such as described here, can contribute much to a lecture on a certain subject. Yet it is only one out of a wide range of aids to help lecturers illustrate a talk.

►

Blackboard or flannelboard? Distraction or concentration?

The main element—and this has been proved many times over—is that the speaker must know how to use it. If inappropriately used, there are times when a flannelboard demonstration can harm a lecture rather than be of positive value. And the preparation of such a demonstration takes much more time than the talk itself. How many speakers can afford the luxury of such time-consuming preparatory work?

Admittedly, a talk which will have to be given on more than one occasion would warrant such well-founded preparation. And there are certain types of talks which could be illustrated practically only by this kind of visual aid—such as talks on a manufacturing process of a factory assembly line for example. In such a context the speaker must build up element after element of the process so that his audience can grasp the whole and the implications at all stages. Here the advantage over the classic chart or graph lies in the fact that the audience virtually sees the process develop. The listener automatically follows the speaker instead of—as in the use of a chart—being distracted by something which is not of immediate concern and consequently missing what has been said. The fact that some students have quicker comprehension than others and are often ahead of the speaker can sometimes constitute a disturbing, if not detrimental, element in teaching. The flannelboard keeps such hazards to a minimum, ensuring that the students progress at the same pace.

The flannelboard should not be used to show statistical data. In the latter case, it is the " understanding at a glance " which counts, not the sometimes laborious construction of the " image ".

The flannelboard works mostly with symbols, not with " real " pictures. A concrete subject is hard to demonstrate by symbols, an abstract one much easier. We all remember the charts seen during our school-days, let us say about the functioning of the human ear. Everybody knows what the human ear looks like—so why invent a symbol for it? The ear, on the contrary, could serve as a symbol for " hearing " in a flannelboard demonstration. But when it comes to the functioning of the ear, we had best show an enlarged diagram of that part of the head—for which there is no symbol.

The symbols for each demonstration must not only be well chosen, they must also be designed in such a way that people at the back of a medium-sized room can readily see what they signify. And again there are certain limitations in the use of a flannelboard: because of its size, it is restricted to relatively small audiences, say groups of up to fifty.

A lecturer must be familiar with these and other restrictions of the flannelboard before using it. As a matter of fact, he may run into a rather sophisticated group which, when seeing this kind of demonstration, may refuse it on the ground that it looks somewhat like an explanation designed for ten-year old children. The group may say that its intellectual level was under-estimated by the speaker and that an audience composed of trade union instructors for instance cannot be handled like the union members whom they are supposed to teach. A group of this kind might take a stand which could make it extremely difficult for the lecturer to pass the crucial point at which an audience is willing to accept the fact that they are being taught.

There is a further danger: many lecturers, knowing the effectiveness of flannelboard demonstrations with regard to certain kinds of subjects, will become too wrapped up in their use and try to perfect them even more than need be. Such a speaker may try to be something of a magician, concentrating on the " technique " rather than on the subject. If all goes well, the audience will tend to regard him as a good comedian but will never take him seriously. The substance of the talk gets lost. In the end, the audience is disappointed and will rightly ask itself what it has actually learnt. The sole ability to master a certain technique and to be amusing as well never make a good speaker.

Some kinds of subjects, of an abstract nature, will lend themselves very well to the flannelboard technique. Such subjects, usually referred to as dry, become more easily intelligible, and the speaker can save much effort by showing something concrete to the audience. The speaker must be able to judge the moment at which he should resort to the use of audio-visual aids. Only experience can help here. With regard to the flannelboard, this is particularly true. Every speaker

A Flannelboard

... or feltboard is – as its name specifically indicates – a board covered with flannel cloth or felt. There are two possible arrangements: either the flannel is spread or pasted permanently onto a board of about 80 by 120 cms (the board being of plywood or other light material or plastic and preferably framed to protect the edges), or the cloth is merely a piece of flannel brought along by the instructor when lecturing away from his normal base. To meet the latter temporary measure, the piece of cloth should preferably be affixed to the wall or, failing this, put on any other flat support such as a wooden door, generally available in any classroom and detachable from its hinges at least for a short while.

Symbols, figures, letters or photographs can be stuck on a flannelboard, if pasted on medium-grain sandpaper, such as is used by carpenters to round off edges or smooth the surface of wooden equipment.

Funds permitting, so-called "flock paper" – a light, flexible cardboard produced for this purpose in large, multicoloured sheets and sprayed with plastic fibre on one side – can be obtained at a fairly reasonable cost. The special flock paper has the added advantage that designs can be directly drawn thereon.

The prime advantage of the flannelboard is that symbols can be stuck on, transposed or removed at will by the instructor during the course of his lecture.

must practice this technique before using it, otherwise he runs the risk of meeting endless difficulties.

After perusal of the foregoing, the conclusion may be reached that it would be best to refrain from using this technique and leave it to the gifted and talented lecturers to play with. This idea is tantamount to refusing to learn to swim because of the risk of drowning. In respect of the flannelboard, this would suggest that every speaker should be familiar with the technique, as from time to time an opportunity may arise at which he could effectively use it.

Roughly speaking, this is the attitude adopted today in many countries towards this fairly recent method of demonstration. It may differ in its degree of use depending on the mentality and type of audience, the use of symbols which must be tied to commonly accepted and recognised facts—but the method of using flannelboards of varying size is generally accepted. Almost every educational institution uses or at least knows the flannelboard and its possibilities. Yet, the somewhat reluctant attitude—for reasons such as the ones already described and others—of teachers, educators and lecturers to adapt it to their needs can largely be attributed to the fact that often there is not enough time to prepare a "good show".

C. N. Fernau

ILO's Flannelboard Symbols

In connection with its recent international Seminar on Teaching about the ILO and its Work, held at Geneva in November 1965 and reported on separately in the last issue of Labour Education, *the ILO Workers' Education Branch prepared a set of charts which can be used as a flannelboard demonstration set highlighting a series of themes explaining the purpose, structure and functioning of the International Labour Organisation. The set is printed in the form of a wall sheet exhibition—in such a way that lecturers may cut out individual symbols, mount them on flock paper and use them on the flannelboard. In addition, the demonstration sheets can be used on a flipboard where no flannelboard is available.*

The preparation of this set of visual aids for speakers by the ILO Workers' Education Branch stems in large part from a number of suggestions put forward at its recent meeting of labour educators. Through this medium the Workers' Education Branch not only hopes to contribute to and facilitate the work of speakers, but to help workers' educators all over the world in explaining the many aspects of the work of the I.L.O.

Readers and/or institutions interested in obtaining a set of the above-mentioned audio-visual aids free of charge are invited to apply to the Workers' Education Branch, International Labour Office, CH-1211 Geneva 22, Switzerland.

▼

Drawing – Encouragement to the Beginner

A worker-educator who uses visual aids during a talk often hears other instructors or lecturers say: "Obviously this is an excellent technique, but it's not one that I can handle: I don't know how to draw." It is true that many educators are discouraged about using visual aids before they even give the problem serious analysis. Let us try to show that, to be sure, visual aids do need imagination and care, but that it is not necessary to have artistic talent and ample resources to create them.

•

First, let us put the problem in its proper setting: educators and psychologists are of the opinion that good visual aids greatly facilitate real understanding of a subject presented orally. But the fact is that workers' education is still most frequently based on the oral presentation, at least as the point of departure for group study. On this account, visual aids can be utilised so often by worker-educators that it is worthwhile giving a careful study of their mechanism.

There are innumerable instruments that we now have at hand: overhead projectors and their accessories, magnetic boards and their little figures, flannelboard and adhesive cardboard, flipcharts and felt-point pens, posters and notice boards, even down to the blackboard with its chalk and eraser, not to mention apparatus which may combine several of these means. Some are expensive; others are cheap. Some are cumbersome; others are easily transportable. Some require electricity; others need only day light. An advantage in one respect is always compensated by some drawback. In the final analysis, all these means afford the same service: to give a visual support to an oral statement. The choice made among them generally reflects the amount of money available and the circumstances in which they will be used – and this latter is a highly important factor. That is to say, a school or college with permanent installations will tend to prefer electrical apparatus which is bulky but perfected, whereas a worker-educator, constantly on the move to visit isolated trade unions, will prefer a blackboard which is to be found virtually everywhere, or the simple visual aids which he can carry in his brief-case and which can be installed with a few nails or thumbtacks on the wall of any room.

Since this article is written by someone who is very bad at drawing, and is written for his comrades in misery in the artistic field, still another serious drawback of the blackboard remains to be mentioned: to use it correctly while giving a talk, without losing contact with the audience, you need a quick artistic eye and talent and a quite special gift for calligraphy. If you do not have these skills, the improvised use of the blackboard while lecturing is not always of positive value. There is no need to dwell on the obscure compositions full of confused details which decorate so many blackboards at the end of otherwise excellent presentations! The overhead projectors and the flipcharts may lead to similar disappointments if their utilisation is improvised, but these instruments, fortunately, have other possibilities. Since this is the case, it is far more preferable to use aids which can be prepared in advance and which are exposed to view with a simple gesture at the exact moment when they are needed. This means, in particular the flannel board and the flipchart (as well as of the overhead projectors, if the necessary installations are available).

Words and pictures

Once the question of equipment is handled in this way, what are we going to offer to the spectators? Two things: words and pictures.

Written texts that can serve as visual aids are usually chapter headings and the key words of a lecture. They help the audience to obtain a clear notion of the structure and also to take meaningful notes. Moreover, these same texts, which remain visible on the board or flipcharts after the lecture is over, often serve as a framework for the discussion which follows. These advantages are significant, but naturally they only apply if the audience knows how to read. On the other hand, the utilisation of texts implies that all the listeners speak the same language: bi-lingual or tri-lingual visual aids would, in practice, be so complicated that they would be more confusing than useful. The choice of texts to be set out visually calls for some thought. Here are a few points to consider: first, they must be short, both to catch the eye of the audience, and also because the available surface is limited. Next, since they are accompanying an oral presentation, there is no need for them to give a complete idea, as for example, a poster ought to do. Lastly, the visual aid must be adapted to the style of the speech and the speech must take the visual aids into account; this two-way adjustment is essential, and at the beginning it involves a certain discipline on the part of the speaker. As has been said above, the flannel board and the flipchart are particularly helpful in linking and synchronising visual aid with the development of the presentation.

You cannot just toss off text designs that are usable, but still it is not necessary to call upon the services of a professional designer. Two pencil lines make it possible to fix a regular height for the letters, which are then sketched in lightly with a pencil; lastly, go over the letters with a felt-point pen, and in this way, with a little practice, you get a readable and esthetically acceptable text. One important detail: black capital letters on a white paper must be at least 4 centimetres high to be legible at ten metres in a good light. I'll simply jog memory here as to the advantage of the use of various colours yields (using felt pens or adhesive cardboards). They can set off the several parts of a talk, or perhaps the pro and con arguments, or perhaps distinguish the main ideas from the dependent ones. On the black base of a feltboard, light coloured cardboards (yellow and white) are the most striking; on the light background of a flipchart, black or red ink will give the best contrast.

Various graphic drawings and symbols can be utilized, like the above texts, to lend visual emphasis to an oral presentation. The ways of using them are similar. They are particularly useful when dealing with an illiterate audience, or in mixed language groups, with interpretation.

The use of graphs to illustrate statistical data does not pose any problems which are basically different from those involving texts. You will nearly always find a simple model to follow in a book or magazine and the job itself is a matter of using a ruler, a pencil, an eraser and a felt pen, as described above.

Within the reach of everybody

On the other hand, the choice and the actual drawing of designs raise quite special problems which need to be looked into more carefully in order to point out, at the sime time, the simplicity, the difficulties and the pitfalls.

The designs which are technically the most simple are valuable, if they are understandable by the audience. Here, for example, are faces, people and objects proposed by the Bulletin of the Central Bureau of Workers' Education in India (September 1967), (figure 1) and by the French C.G.T. to an educators' seminar in October 1967 (figure 2). This type of design is within the reach of everybody. In addition, it should not be forgotten that there are many ways of copying more complicated drawings if you do not feel up to the job of drawing from your imagination. The simplest is tracing. If, for instance, you need to enlarge an illustration in a book to a size that will go on a flipchart, there are various means: a projector throws the illustration from the book onto the flipchart, and you trace around the outlines with a pencil. It is also possible to photograph the illustration on a slide, and project it onto the flipchart. Finally, you can make a grid of small squares with a light pencil on the illustration, and a similar grid of large squares on the flipchart and then measure off the illustration onto the pad, larger but with identical proportions, working square by square. The carrying-over of the image is then greatly facilitated. Still another system is to cut out the drawings used on posters and to make a series of them for the feltboard (you can see one example of this technique in No. 9 of this Bulletin).

As a matter of fact, it is not the execution of the visual symbol which presents the real problem; it is far more the way in which it is conceived or chosen in terms of the visual and cultural habits of the audience. During a recent seminar, one participant asked whether the I.L.O. had drawn up a listing of symbols accepted internationally; such a thing is doubtless possible for highway signals or for certain posters on industrial safety, but in workers' education, the subjects are too subtle and variable to allow for standardization of the symbols that may be used to illustrate them.

Angel: white Devil: black?

Without even speaking of international codification, simply going from one country to another sometimes leads to strange misinterpretations, as the time when a filmstrip was projected in Africa, one image of which represented a good trade unionist, symbolized as an angel, and a bad man symbolized as a devil; but the devil was black, the angel was white! That elicited quite a few remarks from the audience – fortunately more bantering than bellicose – the participants merely stressing that the blacks weren't all devils and the whites could not all be considered angels! Someone has also said that a simplified drawing, in the style of those illustrating this article, would be rather meaningless in certain countries. Someone else has commented that, for those who are not of the British tradition, the judge in his wig, shown in the drawing of our Hindu friends, is likely to be mistaken for a "hippie", and this might lead to certain misinterpretations. But there's no need to exaggerate these difficulties, for, in the long run, the meaning of a visual aid is made clear by the speech which accompanies it. This is merely a further argument in favour of the careful preparation of the visual aids by the person who is going to use them, in the light of what he wishes to teach his audience.

In all events, finding simple illustrations which possess the desired symbolic content is significantly more difficult than writing a number of words of text. With equipment which costs little, like the feltboard and the flipchart you can easily begin with texts and insert illustrations to take their place as soon as any good ideas have come along for this purpose. The game is worth the candle, as is strikingly proved by the figure No. 3, reproduced on page 6, put together by a group of German educators to expound the problems (and the solutions) of a discussion group. Personal idiosyncracies – different approaches, habits, ideas and values of participants in discussion groups are evoked in this picture. There is the solid hedgehog, gaining little and contributing little; the monkey, the extrovert who participates loud and long; the kind, the shy introvert, hesitant to venture a viewpoint. Their fascimiles are found at every meeting. Any worker-educator who lets his imagination go a bit will see in this assemblage of animals the reminder of so many past experiences – amusing or difficult – that with a little reflection, he can give a talk on the psychology of group study.

During a course for teachers, the preparation of visual aids for a speech may be a worthwhile group endeavour. It is a good exercise in pedagogical techniques, and the search for texts and symbols, discussion on them and experiments with them also constitute an indirect means of absorbing the subject matter.

•

Imagination and practice count far more than technique and material equipment in this activity. We should not minimize the effort that a lecturer or an instructor has to make to get out of the ancient rut of making a speech from behind a reading stand, with a sparing use of the blackboard. He has to be looking for ideas for "visualisation" long ahead of time. He has to think of the visual aids in terms of the speech, and the speech in terms of the visual aids. He should put his pride in his pocket and ask the opinion of his friends, go over the speech with them, so that they may (constructively!) criticize the technique. Lastly, he must confront an audience without being completely sure that he will be taken seriously.

All educators have come up against difficulties of this sort. But since we find listeners getting such undeniably superior results from a talk accompanied by visual aids, we should do our utmost to urge that those who are still hesitant should try the experiment. Perhaps later on they will recount their experiences in *Labour Education*, so that we can all draw the appropriate conclusions.

Jean-Jacques Favre

YOU CAN DO THIS, IF YOU TRY! YES, YOU CAN. DON'T BE AFRAID TO DRAW. DRAWING IS NOT ALWAYS A DIFFICULT JOB, IT MAY SOMETIMES BE A FUN. ANY ONE CAN DRAW AN EGG AND MAKE PENCIL STROKES ON PAPER. TAKE A FELT-TIPPED INK-TUBE OR A WAX PENCIL AND A SETSQUARE. DRAW

AN EGG ON A PAPER. ADD A FEW PURPOSEFUL STROKES AND SEE THE CHANGE. EVEN A CHILD WILL BE ABLE TO RECOGNIZE IT IS THE FACE OF A HAPPY MAN. THE MAN CAN BE MADE AGGRIEVED BY CHANGING THE STROKES. HIS MOODS WILL CHANGE WITH THE CHANGING STROKES.

YOU CAN ALSO VERY EASILY AND QUICKLY DRAW STICK FIGURES. YOU CAN MAKE A FIGURE STAND OR WALK OR RUN OR CYCLE.

PUT AN APRON ON HIM AND A SPANNER IN HIS HAND AND HE BECOMES A FACTORY WORKER. THE STICK FIGURES WILL BE AT YOUR COMMAND AND YOU CAN MAKE THEM ACT IN WHATEVER WAY YOU WOULD LIKE TO. HE CAN BE MINER, A WORKER. THERE CAN ALSO BE TWO PERSONS ENGROSSED IN DISCUSSION. SIMILARLY YOU CAN ALSO ILLUSTRATE A GROUP BUSY IN DISCUSSION.

Figure 1

YOU CAN MAKE GOOD USE OF THESE STICK FIGURES IN YOUR LESSONS AND MAKE TEACHING INTERESTING. YOU CAN DRAW THEM ON CHALK BOARD WITH COLOURED CHALKS OR ON BIG BLANK PAPERS-FLIPS. THEY WILL BE BEFITTING SUPPLEMENT TO YOUR VERBAL NARRATIONS. FOR INSTANCE, YOU CAN ADOPT YOUR LESSON ON 'GRIEVANCE PROCEDURE' FOR USING STICK-FIGURES. HERE, OUR FITTER FRIEND RAVI IS FOUND WORKING AT THE MACHINE. HE HAS A GRIEVANCE. HE TALKS IT OVER WITH THE FOREMAN. IN ANOTHER SCENE RAVI'S UNION REQUESTS THE MANAGEMENT FOR VOLUNTARY ARBITRATION. HERE WE FIND TWO MORE STICK FIGURES SYMBOLISING THE UNION AND THE MANAGEMENT. THE THIRD SCENE MAY BE OF CONCILIATION WHERE THE CONCILIATION OFFICER TRIES TO BRING ABOUT SETTLEMENT BETWEEN THE TWO PARTIES. THE FOURTH SCENE IS OF INDUSTRIAL TRIBUNAL WHERE THE CASE IS HEARD AND THE AWARD IS GIVEN

IN ALL, WE FIND A FITTER A FOREMAN, A UNION REPRESENTATIVE A MANAGEMENT S REPRESENTATIVE, A CONCILIATOR AND A JUDGE—REPRESENTED IN STICK FIGURES. SIMILARLY YOU CAN ALSO ILLUSTRATE OTHER TOPICS WITH STICK FIGURES AND MAKE LESSONS INTERESTING. DON'T HESITATE TO TRY YOUR HAND ON THE CHALK BOARD. PRACTICE MAKES A MAN PERFECT!

WOKER'S' EDUCATION NAGPUR, INDIA. SEPTEMBER 1967

Figure 1 (cont.)

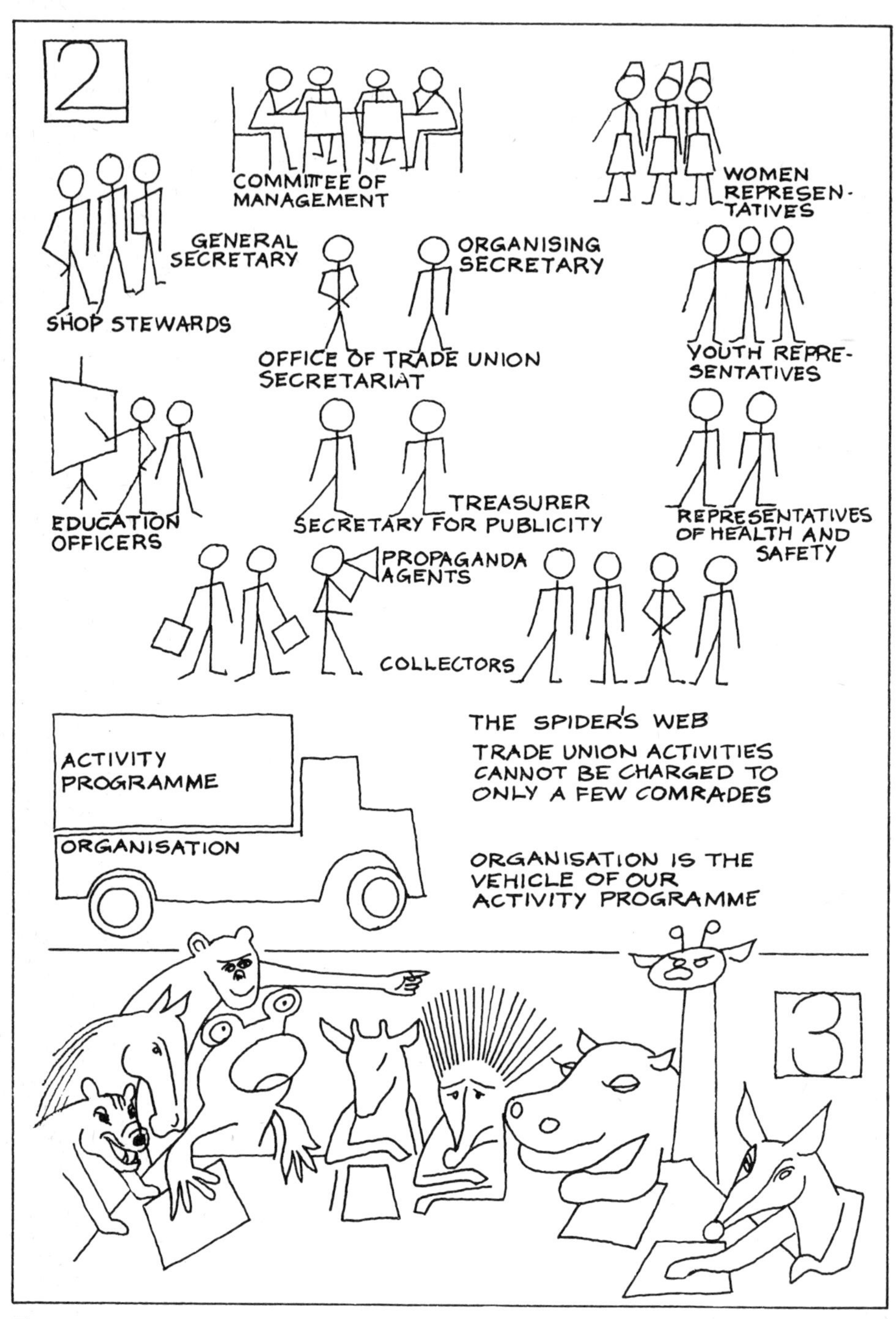

Figure 2

Figure 3

Blackboard, Flipchart and Flannelboard

Jean-Jacques FAVRE
Workers' Education Branch

In circles concerned with workers' education, we frequently discuss audio-visual aids. Yet it is evident that too few are those who use competently such simple aids as the flannelboard, the flipchart or even the blackboard. This may frequently be due to a misconception of their proper use and to the fact that sufficient time is not taken in preparing their proper utilisation.

•

Also one sometimes asks from these tools what they cannot give and one does not use them where they are specially suitable. This is regrettable because they are cheap and simple tools with which tailor-made aids can be prepared for each course or group session. This close adaptation to each theme or educational action is most valuable. It should sometimes lead one to prefer these tools to ready-made posters, films or filmstrips which are undoubtedly more striking but which are impossible to adapt to precise educational requirements arising during the presentation of a given subject to a given group of whose background the artist or producer has no prior knowledge.

It may rightly be said that the overhead projector or the episcope offers a similar adaptability and a more striking presentation. However—considering the regrettably modest purse and heavy luggage of so many workers' educators—this type of equipment does not come within the category of low cost or light weight, nor does it have the robust simplicity of the flannelboard and flipchart.

It may therefore prove useful to relate some experiences recently made in a labour education seminar held in Chtaura, Lebanon. These experiences were modest in terms of scope and material involved, but their value may be gauged from the fact that participants several times declared that the methods used had made it easier for them to study and discuss the subjects of the programme.

Both a lecture and group discussion were foreseen on ILO Conventions and Recommendations, dealing with their preparation, implementation and application, as well as measures taken by Arab countries in this context. The subject was of evident interest for trade union leaders and educators at the seminar but—no less evidently—the presentation by a lecturer and the assimilation by his audience of the principles, statistics and administrative mechanism involved pointed to a dry and complex topic from which minds would be liable to wander.

[1] *See* **Labour Education,** *No. 7.*

The lecturer had no film or filmstrip dealing with the subject; however he had three posters [1], various statistical elements found in ILO publications, and some concrete cases provided by the competent Application of Standards Branch.

The posters dealt with the administrative mechanism, and the artist who composed them had happily foreseen the possibility of cutting them up for use on a **flannelboard**. The lecturer decided to avail himself of this possibility and built up the flannelboard set illustrated on page 38. There were two reasons for this: first, he was scheduled to give only one talk on the subject, and therefore a continuous visual presentation of the application procedure appeared to him better than three separate posters; in the second place, the flannelboard technique enabled him to synchronise the development of the illustration with his own speech—a more effective method than placing all the poster illustrations on the wall as a prelude to the talk.

For the reader's convenience, the illustration symbols have been numbered and a very brief explanation is appended. These were not used at the Chtaura seminar, the relevant part of the talk providing detailed comment of the symbols as they were placed one by one on the board. The quasi-complete absence of written text readily facilitated simultaneous interpretation of the French-language exposé into English and Arabic without loss of substance.

Incidentally, such material, once established, can be repeatedly used and thus justify more fully the pains taken in its preparation: the instructor dealt with the same topic a few weeks later in Malta, having recourse to the same flannelboard with suitably adapted comments, and recorded an equally favourable response as in Lebanon.

•

The **flipchart**, in turn, proved useful at the Chtaura seminar to provide a general appreciation of the trends and results concerning the ratification of ILO Conventions and of the measures taken by Arab countries in this sphere. A series of simple graphs had been prepared showing, first, the relative evolution in the number of member States, of Conventions and of Ratifications; secondly, the Conventions ratified by Arab state members in comparison with the over-all average of ratifications per member State; and thirdly, the number of ratifications given to the "right of man" Conventions (freedom of association, discrimination and forced labour) as compared to the number of ratifications of the average Convention. These graphs and charts had been very simply prepared on white paper with felt markers of two or three colours; they impressed on participants trends and proportions rather than precise statistics, which was all that was needed. No reproduction is given of these charts here, for the simple reason that they were consumed by the recent ILO annex fire and there has been no time as yet to reproduce them. We know at least one reader who will be relieved : the smiling Lebanese participant for whom statistics may appear to trace the rainbow, but usually contrive to hide the pot of gold!

•

Let us now turn to the **blackboard**. Towards the end of the Chtaura seminar, two work groups were asked to list the main workers' education subjects directly or indirectly related to the ILO, with an indication of the categories of trade unionists to whom these subjects had to be taught, as well as the methods, material and duration planned. This assignment implied the synthesis of various elements and had to be carried out without previous preparation. The use of the blackboard made it far easier: thus, for instance, the French-speaking group started its discussion in front of a blackboard bearing only the abovementioned headings and vertical columns [1]. Starting mainly from the topics to be taught, and with frequent flashbacks and digressions, the group explored the subject and finally managed to cover most of its essential aspects. As discussion progressed, the group leader made succinct notes on the board of the main ideas arising from the exchange. As the illustration shows, by the end of the session, the blackboard was nearly filled with indications grouped in a much more logical order than had been the case during the discussion. The blackboard content had thus been compiled with the agreement of the group before their very eyes. Then the board was transferred to the main conference hall and used by one of the participants to present orally a well-planned and complete report of the group findings which were later recorded by photograph.

•

[1] *See* **Labour Education,** *Nos. 6 and 7.*

[1] *See cover photo of this Bulletin.*

A word about the materials used. The blackboards had been found locally—as is nearly always the case—and were of the ordinary school type. The flannelboard consisted of a plain piece of cloth looped on one side for wall suspension on nails or thumbtacks, and taking up no more room than a shirt in a suitcase. The flipchart, slightly heavier, comprised sheets of thick paper with a strong cardboard cover, the latter folding back and serving as a stand. The author of the present article considers it important that the three tools be independent one from the other, as this allows their simultaneous use. Certain models currently on sale combine all three on one stand; in that way only one tool can be used at a time; furthermore, if the flipchart is of the right size, blackboard and flannelboard are too small to be convenient.

●

In closing, let it be emphasised again that this article does not claim to be exhaustive nor does it reveal anything new. Its purpose has been to recall to mind the existence of certain very simple and readily accessible educational tools and to typify their effective use. The very positive reaction obtained on the too few occasions when they have been used more than justifies the present mention. With a little imagination, time and at small cost, workers' educators can find in these simple tools the means of notably improving the educational impact of their teaching. Additional technical and other data can be provided upon request to ILO Workers' Education Branch.

A Word about Posters

What?

Talking about posters one may mean different things. These things may differ in shape, in size, in colour, and of course may have been designed for a different purpose. They come as posters properly speaking, but also as charts, diagrams, flipcharts, etc. But always they are static graphic presentations of an idea, a structure or a situation. They are composed of text, text and illustration or illustration only. The text is usually short, the image [part] impressive, convincing, easily intelligible. Or it isn't a good poster.

Additional effects can be added at additional cost: colour. As means of communication they convey a message which sticks in the minds of those who see them. In some way or other, posters should influence or educate.

What for?

Educational posters come alone or in series. In the latter case they must be coherent; or at least treat an identical subject. Coherence can also be achieved by using posters as visual aids in lecturing.

Posters can announce an event. They carry news, either in the proper sense of the word or in that they convey new ideas. Posters can be a form of artistic expression, although they are not in most cases. However, some of those made by great artists such as Toulouse-Lautrec today fetch five-figure prices at auctions.

Posters are visual aids in stressing certain important points. In this way they contribute to change behaviour or stimulate changes of existing social or other structures. Publicity makes use of this fact to induce potential customers to buy certain products even if customers do not feel in need of such products immediately.

Posters make people think, make people aware or remind them of facts they may have momentarily forgotten.

Posters, especially charts and diagrams, correlate several facts or tendencies and thus facilitate a fuller understanding of a given situation.

Posters are "two dimensional" and, therefore, not the "real thing". They leave way for human imagination. This is important when considering the graphic concept and determining the printing process so as to make posters visual aids and not visual obstacles for the communication of an idea.

How?

Posters are usually printed by various processes: offset or letter-press for larger quantities, silkscreen, lithography or photographic processes for smaller numbers.

They are made available on paper or cardboard of varying qualities. But they can also be produced by hand on any of these materials as well as on wood, sheet metal, cloth, or they can be painted on a house's wall – meant to stay there until rain washes them off.

Once prepared or printed, posters can be used again and again, provided that care is taken in storing them between uses.

Who?

Every workers' educator can make his own posters, charts or diagrams – even if he does not think very highly of his proficiency as designer or draftsman.

Every educator can put them to use in his classroom. Having prepared these visual aids for his teaching beforehand saves him the trouble to draw illustrations on the black board while in class and gives him more time to concentrate on his actual teaching. The poster makes out of the educator a methodi-

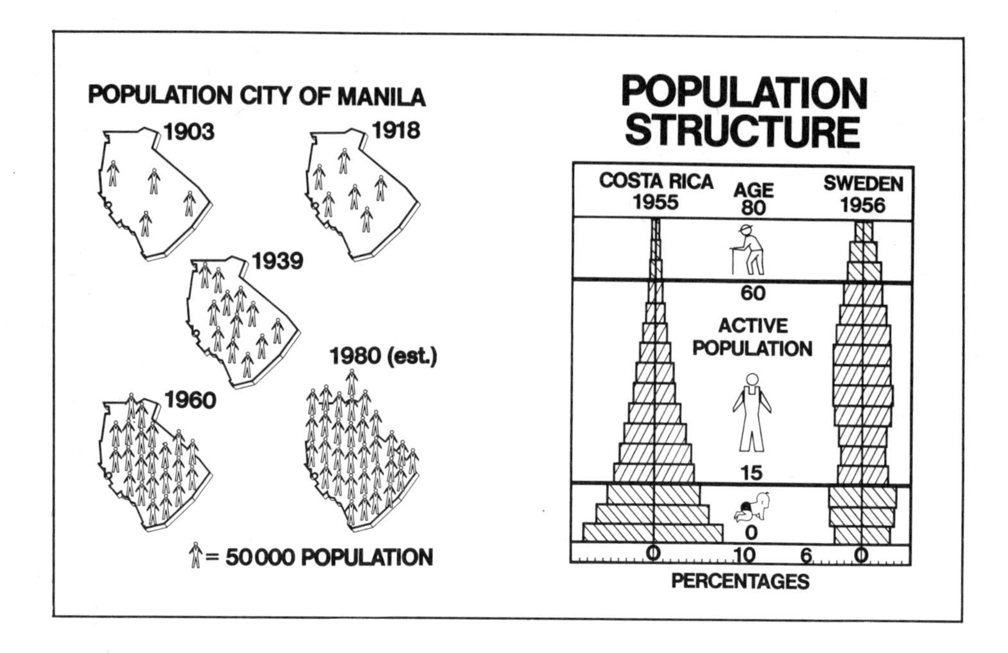

cal "explainer" who needs no or only a few notes from which to teach, as the poster gives him the same services as speakers' notes would. To some extent, posters might even educate the educators to stick more closely to their subjects.

Using posters, the educator expresses his train of thought through an aid which strengthens his message. This, on the other hand, makes his teaching more lively. He thus increases the efficiency of his teaching.

The learner will understand better if he hears the explanation accompanying a graphic design.

The educator may wish to use a diagram to illustrate a complicated system or structure. The learner, however, may react adversely to too many details given to him simultaneously at one time. In this case it may be wise to conceal parts of the graphic display and reveal them to the class only in stages as the teacher talks about them.

Storage

Posters, especially the printed types, are costly to produce. In order to ensure repeated use, they must be stored properly. They ought to be kept flat either hanging or, if space permits, laid flat. The edges could be reinforced with transparent adhesive tape to avoid tear.

The use of posters in workers' education is old hat. Yet, nothing new has been invented to replace this visual aid so that there is always a demand for it. Unions print them for their outdoor campaigns or indoor educational activities. Some examples of such posters are depicted on these pages. Some are promotional, others educational in nature. Some hand-made flipcharts illustrate the fact that posters can be rudimental as regards their execution, but still be effective as teaching aids.

Once more the Workers' Education Programme of the ILO has published a set of flipcharts or posters on "The stake of workers' in population questions". The set is composed of thirteen posters, six blank sheets for diagrams reflecting more local aspects to be added by the lecturer in case of need, and twelve pages of text introducing and explaining the posters on the basis of which an instructor can develop his lecture.

Requests for a limited number of free-of-charge sets may be addressed to the ILO.

Curt Fernau

The following text has been taken from "Syndicalisme", No. 1322, review of the French Democratic Confederation of Labour.

MAKE YOUR OWN POSTERS!

The principle underlying silk-screening is simple. It is a matter of passing ink through a silk screen at selected places (representing letters or a design), this ink being then deposited on a sheet of paper.

So much for the theory. Next comes the practice. What is said here has to do with the simplest lay-out. Once learned, it can be refined and hence perfected.

❶ Buy or make a very rigid wooden frame which will not warp. For example, use brace-laths 80 × 80. Assemble it solidly. The most usual size (inside measurements) is 60 cm × 80 cm.

❷ The screen is traditionally of silk. But now-a-days there are special cloths of tergal which are quite cheap. It is important to choose wisely the grain of the screen (i.e. the size of the mesh) in terms of the work to be done.

❸ Assemble the screen and the frame. Avoid putting in too many nails. Use them only to stretch the cloth tightly before gluing it with a coating of cellulose, then strengthening it on the frame with broad bands of adhesive paper.

❹ Mount the frame thus obtained by means of hinges onto a bearing surface of hard material (wood, plexiglass, etc.), the hinges allowing the frame to be removed easily for cleaning.

❺ To "prepare" the screen, draw directly on the cloth inside the frame the text or illustration. Do this with a brush, using DRAWING GUM. Let it dry. To make this preparation really successful, it is preferable to draw a full-sized templet pattern and slip it underneath the cloth.

❻ Then spread over the whole screen a cellulose filling lacquer, using a squeegee or "doctor".

❼ To make the screen "come through", the drawing gum on which the cellulose lacquer has not stuck must then be removed. To do so, rub the cloth with a bit of cotton waste soaked in oil of turpentine until the ink has gone. This is checked visually. The parts of the cloth which represent the text or the drawing must have their mesh transparent. The rest of the screen must be blocked up, to keep the ink from passing through it. Now the screen is ready.

❽ Place some sheets of paper under the frame and apply the ink. For this, you need a squeegee having the width of the inside of the frame (a wooden plate fitted with a rubber edge), and special ink, for example "SERINK", to which is added some "extender-base" or "retarder" to make it sufficiently fluid and to avoid its drying too quickly.

❾ The first sheets are wasted. Once the ink passes well everywhere – and not too much! – one or two sweeps of the squeegee will be enough to print a sheet.

❿ Hang the sheets up to dry on wash-lines with clothes-pegs. A big headache! for you need plenty of space....

⓫ If you want, later on, to make a fresh printing, remove the maximum of ink with an old rag. Then clean off the screen with a special solvent.

⓬ If you want to get back to a completely blank screen: remove the ink and in addition clean off from the screen the cellulose lacquer, using a special solvent (acetone). If it is thoroughly cleaned, a screen can be utilised very many times.

N.B.:

- To make a poster in two colours, proceed in the same way as shown above, but do it twice, as if for two different posters. Once for the black, once for the colour. For this, you should prepare an accurate pattern or stencilplate, with the necessary careful registering.
- Although the process is quite simple, it is possible that you will not succeed at the first try. It calls for delicate handling and an exact feeling for what is needed in the way of laquer or of ink.

Sketch No. 1: mounting the silk (1 gluing, 2 cutting the silk, 3 placing and sticking bands of "Kraft" paper to delimit the desired size. – Sketch No. 2: mounted frame. – Sketch No. 3: printing.

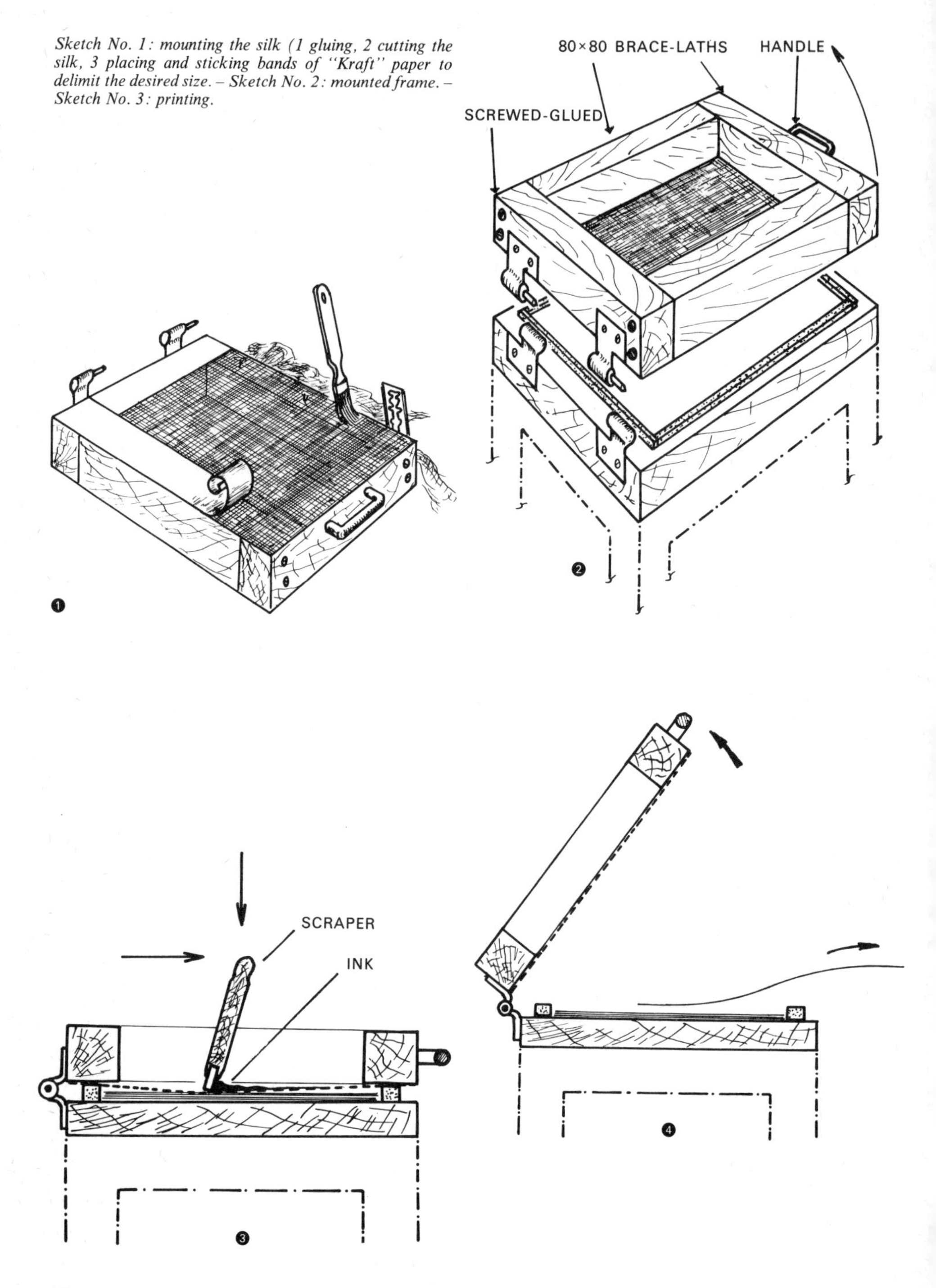

The overhead projector: description and use

One of the modern educational tools whose use is becoming more widespread in workers' education centres and colleges is the overhead projector. It is sometimes known as the " white board ", in contrast to the blackboard with which it has certain features in common.

A brief description of the projector and its possible uses may be of guidance to those of our readers who are contemplating buying one. The Bulletin will gladly give space to readers who may wish to relate their concrete experiences in handling this apparatus and illustrate original ways and means of putting it to effective use.

•

As may be seen from the sketch, the overhead projector consists of a small transparent writing slab, a high-powered bulb under this base and a combination of lens and mirror placed just above the instructor's head. By means of the apparatus, notes made by the instructor on the slab are immediately projected onto a screen behind him and facing the audience. The projection is in the form of a square which, at a distance of approximately two metres, may vary in size between 1 and 2.50 metres depending on the type of model used. The luminosity is such that the projector may be used either in daylight or in semi-darkness. In general, the apparatus measures 60 × 30 × 30 cms. and weighs between 15 and 20 kg. It can be used either on an ordinary table or, as is more convenient, on a mobile trolley to facilitate transportation within the lecture room or from one room to another.

Some of the advantages and drawbacks of the projector may already be apparent from this brief general description. The machine projects behind the speaker notes or sketches made by him on the transparent slab while facing his study group; there is therefore no risk of the instructor losing contact with his audience as may happen when obliged to turn his back to write on a blackboard. The apparatus reproduces normal-sized script or drawings; this is easier than copying, with arm raised, titles or drawings on an enlarged scale onto a blackboard. The screen is so placed that the instructor is rarely interposed between the text to be projected and the audience. It may happen in the course of writing that his hand will cast a vague shadow on the screen. Lastly, the apparatus can be used in daylight conditions, or at any rate in a room light enough for the students to take notes; this is an asset which is not without importance, especially in hot climates where ventilation does not have to be suppressed.

On the other hand, it has to be admitted that the apparatus is heavy, bulky and somewhat cumbersome. If used for prolonged periods in a somewhat dimly lighted room the rather intense luminosity under the transparent base may cause eyestrain and induce fatigue for the instructor.

So far we have considered only the case of an instructor writing and drawing on the projector base, as he would on a blackboard during a lecture.

In practice there are many more versatile and complex uses to which the apparatus may be put, if the writing or drawing is done on a removable sheet of cellophane placed over the transparent base. Most models do in fact incorporate a long roll of thick transparent cellophane mounted on two rollers, the width of the writing slab. When turning the rollers, the cellophane slides over the base somewhat like a film in a camera. The instructor may write on the cellophane with a grease pencil in the manner indicated. Instead of erasing the written material as he would on a blackboard, the cellophane is wound round and the instructor may continue his demonstration on a clean surface. This progressive method has the additional and at times welcome advantage that the texts or drawings can be prepared in advance and then shown to the audience at the appropriate moment. It also allows the intructor to retrace his steps and review something he has already shown. Swivel or sliding blackboards have like advantages to a certain extent, but their possibilities are obviously more limited.

Incidentally, the movable transparent cellophane onto which the subject matter to be projected is transcribed need not necessarily be mounted on rollers. It may also consist of separate sheets similar in size to the transparent base. An additional advantage of individual sheets is that they can be stacked in readiness by the instructor to give the audience a step by step picture of a particular diagram or plan to which he may wish to draw attention in the gradual development of his theme. Another variation is the use of photocopies on a transparent background: a complicated form, for example, may be slid under the roll of cellophane and projected on the screen; the instructor may then fill in the form by writing on the cellophane, and repeat the demonstration anew simply by winding on the cellophane across the transparent form.

Some overhead projectors have an attachment whereby it is possible to project small slides. Those wishing to do this should make sure beforehand that background lighting is not too bright.

The widely varying and combined uses to which both roll and sheet cellophane may be put in utilising the projector offer far greater possibilities than a mere blackboard. In the field of labour education interesting experiments have been made with the use of overhead projectors, particularly for training in economic subjects (the study of productivity, for example). The cost and unwieldy bulk of the apparatus restrict its use, practically speaking, to colleges or institutes with permanent facilities and an extensive and varied syllabus. In such circumstances it is possible for the instructor, with a minimum of practice and preparation, to derive immense value from its use in training programmes.

Jean-Jacques Favre

Filmstrips and Slides

Its is natural for administrators and instructors in charge of workers' education programmes to be on the look-out for technical improvements to enhance and enliven the teaching given. Such improvements should not, of course, be too costly.

Among the teaching aids which may be considered as involving only a modest outlay are filmstrips and slides. To derive maximum benefit from these, it is important to be fully familiar with the various possibilities which they open up as well as the ways in which they may be used. If need be, their use may necessitate adaptation of the course to the filmstrip or slide used ; at times, it is precisely here that the experienced educator may encounter considerable difficulty.

While the following few remarks are by no means exhaustive, they may nevertheless be helpful to those who are thinking of acquiring and making regular use of filmstrips and slides and the necessary projection equipment.

●

A Glance at Equipment Needs

Slides are individual photographs on a transparent mount for projection on a screen; the usual format is 24×36 mm. A *filmstrip* may be said to be a series of " stills " on a single strip, their size likewise being 24×36 mm. as a rule, or sometimes 18×24 mm.

The choice of projectors is so vast as to defy description. From the point of view of the workers' education instructor, it is advisable to select a projector which can show both slides and filmstrips and thus avoid financial outlay on two separate machines. Since the same picture often has to be kept on the screen for a certain length of time, the projector should be equipped with a cooling fan. Finally, if it is planned to use the projector sometimes for small groups and at other times for large audiences, it is advisable that it should have an intensive source of light and an interchangeable lens—features which are well worth the supplementary expenditure. Automatically operated slide projectors, on the other hand, cannot as a general rule be used to show filmstrips and are thus much less interesting from a workers' education point of view.

Filmstrips and sets of slides are generally supplied either with an accompanying booklet giving a written commentary, or with a record or magnetic tape. *To play back a magnetic tape a tape-recorder will be necessary, while a gramophone record calls for the availability of a record-player*. This adds somewhat to the cost of the equipment, but the type of tape-recorder or record-player generally required for workers' education purposes is not exorbitantly expensive. There are, moreover, many other uses to which this equipment may be put so as to justify the initial expenditure. Furthermore, being in fairly common use, such items can frequently be had on loan.

There exist machines which combine projector and record-players, as well as devices which synchronise the playing of a magnetic tape with the projection of slides. Such refinements generally make the apparatus more delicate to handle; while facilitating one operation they tend to restrict somewhat the other uses to which the equipment may be put.

A final word on *screens*. Here again, no one model combines all the advantages. Workers' education training is often given in premises where there is no projection room, and brings together student groups unfamiliar with the more traditional study techniques. This would seem to tip the balance in favour of " non-directional " screens, in plastic for example, rather than glossy screens which give a brighter image to persons sitting directly in front but less so to those sitting to the side. Before making a choice it is a good idea to have a look also at screens designed for projection in daylight conditions: translucid screens with back projection or shaded screens; the drawback to these is that they are rather too " directional ". Of course, there are times when there is no alternative but to project the image on to a white wall or a sheet. Here, again, the fact cannot be overlooked that the commercial cinema has made audiences harder to please.

Educational Value of Filmstrips and Slides

Putting this equipment to good use sets the instructor certain problems and calls for a certain degree of adaptation in both programme and methods. He may with good reason ask himself whether the game is worth the candle when he already has a blackboard and can readily borrow a 16 mm. projector and a few films. Briefly, some of the advantages to be derived are as follows:

- Filmstrips and slides allow a group to examine in common a document or a photo which would otherwise have to be shown to them individually and be liable to incur a falling off of concentration detrimental to the work of the group.
- This type of equipment has greater educational value than films because the screen pictures are " stills "; they may be examined and discussed at the discretion of the instructor.
- Projection magnifies pictures, gives improved technical finish and permits of more detailed examination than is feasible with drawings made or pinned on a blackboard by the instructor during a lesson. It has the additional advantage of repetition as desired, whereas a blackboard chalk drawing is necessarily short-lived.

There are three main types of projection aids which may be combined in a single series while conveying a different message : ***photography*****—giving detailed and as a rule objective pictures (of a country, a factory, a machine, etc.) ;** ***graph*** **or** ***diagram*****—presenting abstract data (statistics, plans, etc.) in relation to theoretical studies; artistic drawing or caricature—illustrating particular aspects of a talk. These different forms of projection are useful auxiliary tools in the treatment of a specific idea or topic.**

In the case of certain subjects note-taking is essential, and this obviously cannot be done in the dark. To surmount this difficulty projection would therefore need to be undertaken in a lighted room; but this entails to some extent diminished concentration when compared with results obtained from projection in complete darkness, not to mention the fact that colour pictures lose their quality in increasing intensity of light. A

Variety of projection (seen from above):

Photography: United Nations headquarters, New York (from the filmstrip " The ILO Story ").

Artistic drawing or caricature: " A lecturer is a man who talks in other people's sleep " (from ILO filmstrip on Methods and Techniques of Workers' Education).

Graph or diagram: " One in the eye is worth two in the ear " (from the above source).

compromise has to be sought: to admit a minimum of diffused light for writing purposes, sufficiently dim not to blot out the projection. From a technical viewpoint, translucid or shaded screens also help to overcome this difficulty. Another solution consists in showing films and slides before the lesson by way of an introduction to the talk, or as a follow-up for the purposes or recapitulation and reminder.

Filmstrips and slides are not identical by any means and in one aspect at least their educational value differs: the filmstrip is a series of pictures neither the number nor the order of which can be altered by the user. This leads some educators to prefer slides, which can be used independently, selected, or at any time transposed to form a new series appropriate to the occasion. It may be argued, on the other hand, that filmstrips are easier to handle and run no risk of topsy-turvy incidents as in the case of slides shown upside down or of pictures in the wrong order bearing no relation whatsoever to the topic under discussion. It is up to the user to weigh the various risks or complications that may be involved.

Another advantage offered by this type of material lies in the fact that the commentary is not necessarily affixed to the picture, as in the case of a sound film for example. Filmstrips and sets of slides are supplied, as already mentioned, with a booklet, a record or a magnetic tape giving the text of a commentary which the producer has specially prepared for use with the pertinent filmstrip or set of slides. The instructor—depending on his personal competence, on the circumstances and amount of time at his disposal—may either use the existing text, modify it to suit his purpose, or introduce comments of his own which he may consider of more appropriate interest to his particular study group. It is indeed very important that the audience clearly grasps the relationship between the picture and the commentary, because the cumulative effect of the two media employed is the very object of the exercise. Should the picture bear no relationship to the commentary, then it will merely prove a distraction. It is also necessary that the students should be able to relate the visual image to their own situation, and this can be achieved more often than not by adapting the commentary to the special circumstances.

Nothing Venture, Nothing Win

For school use, particularly for the teaching of science and technical subjects, there exists a wealth of slides and filmstrips which can be purchased or hired. But in the field of workers' education there is very little material, and what is available is not always suitable for a particular group.

Yet how many people, including the author of this article, are in the habit of carrying a camera around and of inflicting on their relatives and friends interminable showings of pictures—their families at the seaside, their colleagues at the latest congress, or themselves posing in front of historic monuments. These ardent " do-it-yourself experts " among them display a wealth of ingenuity in dubbing these family chronicles, in creating the desired background noises, and in establishing running commentaries. Why not place this enthusiasm and talent at the service of labour education ? For some, an opportunity not to be missed.

If a filmstrip is to be created in a large number of copies, a project of this dimension almost inevitably calls in the early planning stages for the help of professional advisers and technicians in this field, by reason alone of the contemplated distribution, the necessary equipment and the expenditure involved.

If, initially, a start is made by producing an experimental set of slides, then the problem is more one of educational, photographic and artistic techniques than of financial concern. An educational illustration is not the same thing as a holiday snapshot, no more than pedagogic visual material is a chronological travel diary. What is involved is essentially team work between such persons as a workers' education instructor, a photographer and an artist, whom the reader may conceivably find within his own union.

The extent of this article does not make it possible to consider in detail the various operational phases confronting such a team. This aspect can be examined in a subsequent article. Meantime, it will suffice to conclude by stating that in every country there is not a town of any size where an educational institute, an adult educational service or a private educational body has not made an experiment of this kind in its own realm. Their methods and their techniques could certainly be very largely drawn upon by any team willing to embark upon such a venture.

Jean-Jacques Favre

United Kingdom: Introduction to basic economics through television

Mr. F. J. Bayliss, Professor of Industrial Relations in the Department of Adult Education of the University of Nottingham (United Kingdom), in collaboration with a certain number of British educational specialists, recently embarked on an interesting teaching experiment using television combined with a correspondence course. Mr. Bayliss has kindly engaged to summarise the broad lines of this experiment for ILO's "Labour Education" Bulletin.

Television is being rapidly incorporated into education. Schools, colleges and universities all over the world are using it on an increasing scale as a standard aid to teaching. But what part can television play in adult and labour education? How can this new medium of communication be used to bring education to adults who have not been touched by existing methods?

•

To watch or to study

Pupils or college students are members of an educational institution and come together to learn in classes, so television programmes become part of their scheme of teaching. They are watched by groups of students, and teachers plan their courses so that the programmes fit into a co-ordinated pattern. In this way teaching by television becomes part of a larger system and its advantage is that it adds a new dimension to teaching. Similarly, where adults come together to watch television programmes the same advantage applies. After watching a programme, they can, under the guidance of a tutor, discuss it and relate it to what the tutor has been teaching and to their own experience and reading. Television can be incorporated into adult education in this way on the same basis as it has been incorporated into the rest of the educational system.

But the real importance of television for adult and labour education is the fact that television reaches people in their homes. If television can be used for teaching adult and young workers individually at home, then it opens up an entirely new prospect for the promotion of adult education generally.

The basic problem in exploiting this characteristic of television is that television programmes alone can teach the solitary viewer very little. If learning is to be effective, the viewer who wishes to study must actively manipulate ideas and information in writing or discussion, and he must have some means of going back over the material presented to him. This is not to deny that television on its own can stimulate curiosity and a desire to learn, can revise and refresh what has been learnt in the past, can add to what has already been learnt, and these are all important objectives in educational television. But if an adult or young worker is to learn a subject with which he is unfamiliar, he must study it, and viewing television programmes alone is not study. Viewers must have additional aids to study if they are to learn effectively.

So, if adult education is to take advantage of the fact that television reaches individuals in their homes, an aid which is suitable for study at home must be added to television. The correspondence course is the only aid which can be specially designed for students working on their own. By fastening together a series of television programmes and a correspondence course, planned learning can thus be achieved. A correspondence course can provide in book form the same material as the television programmes, so that the student can go back over the ground he has covered until he is familiar with it. Exercises and tests can require him to think about the subject and commit himself to paper, and the marking of his work can bring him into contact with a tutor who, through correspondence, can give him individual guidance.

Economics and Television

On the basis of this line of reasoning the University of Nottingham's Department of Adult Education in collaboration with a television company, produced a series of 13 adult education programmes called ' The Standard of Living—a practical introduction to economics ' for transmission in the Midland region of England. The object of the experiment was to discover what response there would be in terms of numbers of students and in terms of effective self-tuition if adult and young workers were offered television programmes accompanied by a correspondence course.

There was widespread publicity for the course in press advertisements, leaflets distributed through voluntary associations like trade unions and women's organisations, notices in public libraries, and by announcements on the television screen. Although the organisers looked forward to having many casual viewers of the programmes, they were most interested in students who enrolled for the correspondence course. They were charged a nominal fee of 10s., in return for which they got the course handbook and exercises, together with the services of a correspondence course tutor. The exercises were so designed that they could be posted without being put in an envelope and they were postage pre-paid. Some trade unions were especially helpful with recruitment. For example, the Union of Shop, Distributive and Allied Workers, in addition to general publicity, distributed enrolment forms among members known to its Education Department and offered to pay the fees of members who completed the course.

1,400 students took the correspondence course. In addition 1,500 people bought the handbook alone. The enrolled students were 55 per cent. men and 45 per cent. women, with housewives forming 29 per cent. of the total. It is significant that for a course on economics such a high proportion were women. Fifty-six per cent. were under 40 and as many as 11 per cent. under 20. Thirty-eight per cent. had left school at the minimum legal age and 63 per cent. had finished their full-time education at 16 or earlier; 16 per cent. had had higher education. Only one-sixth said that their reason for enrolling was vocational and as many as half said that they had no vocational interest in economics. For the vast majority the subject was entirely new, since less than one-third had ever studied economics before. While two-thirds had received some vocational part-time education, only one in six had ever attended an education class organised by the Workers' Educational Association or a university extra-mural department. The students were, therefore, predominantly new to adult education and new to the subject; they were interested in economics primarily for some reason other than its relation to their job; they were drawn from the whole community in terms of sex, age and educational background.

The programmes, each of 20 minutes, were transmitted weekly on Sunday mornings with a repeat on Monday mornings. Students were advised to watch the programme, read the matching chapter in the handbook, and complete the exercise at one sitting. It had been assumed that all three stages could be completed in about one hour, but many students spent considerably longer than that each week. The exercices had to be posted by a fixed time each week because of the weekly incidence of the programmes. The student has his marked exercise returned together with a checksheet and his tutor's comments.

Economics was chosen as the subject for the experiment because it is of great importance in adult education, especially trade union education. An understanding of basic economic concepts is essential to informed discussion and action in politics and in industrial affairs. It is a subject which is closely related to the everyday experience of adults whether they be workers, housewives, or managers, and it is a subject which large numbers of people holding positions of responsibility, both at work and in the community at large, can put to use when they are called upon to make decisions.

The sort of person for whom the course was intended was a shop steward wanting to know more about incomes policy, or an active member of a women's organisation concerned about rising prices, or a manager interested in arguments about productivity, or an active member of a political party eager to understand the balance of payments. Indeed, the programmes were designed for the active, responsible citizen in all walks of life, on whom the vigour and quality of the democratic life of the community depends.

Although economics is relevant to mature citizenship, it is difficult to teach because it is a subject which does not lend itself to piecemeal treatment. An understanding of one part of the subject tends to depend on understanding the other parts, and it is difficult to pull out particular topics and teach them in isolation. Yet it was intended that students should get to grips with some theoretical concepts and not be given merely descriptive material. So it was decided to make the Keynesian theory of income determination the centre of the course. The early programmes showed how personal experience fitted into a pattern by analysing national expenditure, and they also presented the idea that the output, income and expenditure of the community are simply different aspects of the same flow of wealth. Programmes which dealt with concepts —capital, investment, consumption and saving— followed, and these culminated in a programme about changes in the national income which presented the central features of the Keynesian theory. The theory was then applied to general problems in programmes on demand inflation, full employment and productivity, cost inflation, and the balance of payments. The last three programmes dealt with major problems facing the British economy—economic expansion, manpower and production, and the balance of payments and economic growth.

The course was based on the belief that students should be introduced to elementary economic theory before they are plunged into arguments about contemporary economic policy. The success of this approach depended on the possibility of convincing students that it was worth their while persisting with the earlier, more theoretical, programmes because they would eventually illuminate the later, policy-oriented, programmes. The correspondence course was essential to this success because its exercises enabled students to know that they were achieving mastery of the subject. Each week, having watched the programme and read the matching chapter in the handbook, they completed an exercise which, by using true/false and multiple-choice tests, as well as open-ended questions, took them through a planned process of checking their understanding of the material. When their exercise was returned, it was accompanied by a checksheet giving corrections of their mistakes and by the tutor's comments on their progress.

One of the claims made for the course is that the combination of television programmes with a correspondence course make possible a thorough and moderately theoretical introduction to economic issues. The proof of the pudding was in the eating: 48 per cent. of the students who enrolled completed every exercise and 78 per cent. completed three quarters or more of the exercises.

But the purpose of understanding theory was to use it to illuminate problems. The main way in which the links between theory and practice were brought to students' attention in almost all of the programmes was by giving an expert an opportunity to say how the economic analysis taught in the programme was used by him in his job. For example, in the programme in investment the managing director of a large company described how he made decisions to invest, in the programme on demand inflation the economic adviser to a bank set out what he considered the best way to control inflation, and in the programme on full employment and productivity the Head of the Economic and Research Department of the Trades Union Congress described trade union policies on productivity. Leading officials of the National Economic Development Council played a large part in the three final programmes which were devoted to discussion of major controversial issues. By presenting the experts to the students, television gave us an opportunity to show how economics is used in practice.

Necessity of a dialogue

Although television enables education to be taken into people's living-rooms, and although a correspondence course can give planned direction to study, the learning process remains impersonal and it is in the interplay of personal discussion between students and tutors that much of the quality of adult education is believed to reside. Yet it is possible to reduce the gap between students and tutors in a correspondence course. Correspondence permits the development of a dialogue between students and tutors, and in correspondence each student gets the undivided attention of his tutor. The tutors were expected to engage their students in discussion on papers and they proved that even in the limited duration of this course standards of adult education can be transferred to a correspondence course. In order to encourage students to feel free to initiate exchanges of opinion beyond the range of the exercises, each student was given a set of ' Query Forms ' on which he could set down any problem which puzzled him and in return he got a full answer from his tutor.

Two opportunities for students to meet their tutors were built into the course. Tutors were allocated students in their own locality and each tutor arranged a meeting place. The first meetings were held mid-way through the course and the second a fortnight before its close. These interludes made it possible to ascertain what were the special difficulties in the material which tutors could use as introductions to teaching sessions. The object of the meetings was to show students what face-to-face adult education was like. It must have been felt that many students enrolled for the course precisely because they could not, or did not want to, attend classes, yet 66 per cent. attended the first meetings and 31 per cent. the second. After the conclusion of the course a week-end school on ' Britain's Economic Situation ' was held at the University of Nottingham and 25 per cent. of the students attended although many had to travel considerable distances and they had to bear the full cost of accommodation. Several conventional education classes in economics have been started among these students and the Workers' Educational Association is endeavouring to draw more of them into its programme of classes. While the success of adult and labour education by television and correspondence course does not depend on students moving on to study in classes, the desire to join a class on the part of some students is an important by-product.

Regular reading is an essential part of study. A correspondence course requires students to read, and to that extent the habit of reading is built into it. The specially written handbook for the course matched the television programmes. The students were advised to read the matching chapter in the handbook after they had viewed the programme, for the handbook took them over the same ground as the programme. A student could complete the exercises successfully without any further reading, but obviously the more determined students wanted to go further. The handbook contained a list of 16 carefully graded textbooks, so that a student could decide which was best suited to his ability and experience as a student. Many students bought or borrowed one of these textbooks, Each student was provided with a set of page references for every textbook and for every programme, so that whatever textbook he had, he could do supplementary reading every week.

Pushing a button

The experiment proved successful. It showed that it is possible to use the great advantages of television—its immediacy, its capacity to present material in a striking visual form, its availability in the home at the turn of a switch—to extend adult education to a new audience. The key seems to be that this new medium for communicating knowledge and ideas must be combined with study and tutoring which is so arranged that the individual student can read and write about, and perhaps discuss, the content of the course in such a way that he makes confident progress and always sees the relevance of what he is learning to his daily life.

Labour Education and Mass Information Media

In the last issue of this Bulletin, a brief summary was given of the conclusions of the Workshop on the Use of Radio and Television in Workers' Education, which met in Geneva at the I.L.O. from 20 to 30 November 1967.

A more detailed analysis of these conclusions is given below.

•

The problem of the use of mass communications media in workers' education is not a simple one. To be sure, radio and television afford almost unlimited possibilities of interesting large groups of the population in the basic notions of economics, in planning and more generally in the political, economic and social life of the country. In this respect, they constitute a powerful factor contributing to understanding and participation. On the other hand, used as they now are, in most cases they are poorly prepared to broadcast any trade union training of a specific sort, and are not without serious disadvantages. One such disadvantage is the "conditioning" referred to by Pierre Galoni, Confederate Secretary of the French C.G.T.-F.O. and a member of the Workshop: political conditioning by news and the like; economic conditioning by advertisements; cultural conditioning by entertainment of a questionable intellectual or artistic value. Lastly, in respect to education, there is the risk that radio and television instruction will lead people to overlook the importance of individual effort, and in the final analysis will often present only a sadly deficient fixed menu. Radio listeners and television spectators are hardly ever allowed to select their meals "à la carte".

Are these reasons sufficient to make us decry the vast educational power shown by radio and television, along with the possibilities they afford in the development of labour education? Understandably enough, the reply of the Workshop participants to this question was a definite "no".

Indeed, while there can be no question of relying fully on radio and television and treating them as the long sought panacea for our educational ills, these two great media of mass communication quite naturally find their place within the general pattern of educational action carried on by the trade unions, and it is up to the latter to derive for their members the lessons that are suitable to trade union perspectives and policies. Radio and T.V., in this context, serve as a source of facts for the trade union movement.

Actually, the educational potential of radio is far from being fully utilised, and as for television, it has hardly begun to achieve results in this respect, even in the most advanced countries. These two potent cultural factors still have to find their place within the general framework of the teaching process, and in addition – this being one of their outstanding characteristics – they involve a close collaboration among many diversified groups: the technical and administrative personnel of radio and television, public authorities, educators, employers, trade unionists and the public as a whole must be active participants. Nor is this the least of the difficulties encountered in developing these methods for the educational field. While the producers need the advice of workers' educators in the preparation of the programmes, it is none the less true that the workers' educators cannot alone ensure the proper presentation of these programmes. Radio and television producers are, moreover, frequently reluctant to work out special programmes addressed to limited groups of listeners or spectators.

•

Traditional teaching methods afford scarcely any possibilities to acquaint the broad masses of workers with the principles of planning and social and economic policy. Workers' education programmes on radio and television, even in those countries where illiteracy is still widespread, can do a great deal to stimulate the interest of workers with regard to economic development. In addition, radio and television offer the possibility of preparing programmes intended to appeal to certain large categories of workers. Educational radio, for example, will reach the most isolated rural workers, whereas television is most appropriate to reach the workers in urban areas.

The experts who met in Geneva made it a point to specify that "the use of radio and television for labour education would tend to stimulate the interest of the worker's family in his occupational problems and concerns, and would help to create support for union policies, as well as for national development".

Are not radio and television, in fact, the best possible media for acquainting the public with the principles and aims of the trade union movement?

The Workshop participants agreed that radio and television could not assume the full measure of their value in the matter of workers' education unless they were sustained by tele- and radio-club groupings within which a more thorough threshing out of the problems could be achieved. On the other hand, the association of T.V. with courses by correspondence gives encouraging results[1].

It might be well to point out here that, although the deliberations of the Workshop took for central theme the utilisation of radio and television in workers' education, other mass media of information, such as the press and the moving picture film, have an important part to play, either directly or as supplements to radio and television broadcasts on workers' education.

The social responsibility of radio and television

There is no doubt gainsaying that radio and television, in their desire to serve the public interest, bear a heavy social responsibility. Science and technology, in fact human knowledge as a whole, are developing at a rapid rate and are constantly modifying the conditions of life and work of the labouring masses. Even apart from workers' education as such, radio and television have a duty to provide information, to popularise science and to educate the public. To do so, they need the collaboration of the great labour organisations, and conversely the trade unions must be able to count on the assistance of radio and television for the development of their own educational activities.

[1] *See* Labour Education, *No. 6, February 1966: United Kingdom: Introduction to basic economics through television.*

A few suggestions

It would be difficult to uphold the argument that all the subject-matter of workers' education lends itself readily to broadcasting by mass information media. The fact is that the questions selected must offer sufficient interest from the social point of view and that they must have something in common with the major problems confronting the world today. Bearing this in mind, the experts, with a view to stimulating the production, broadcasting and utilisation of programmes devoted to workers' education, have suggested the possibility of setting up a standing organisation at the national or regional level, so as to bring together the producers and distributors of radio and television programmes with the trade unionists interested in workers' education, with adult education experts, and in some instances with representatives of the public authorities. Each of these groups could feed information into a central agency which in turn would forward it on to the given national or regional organisation, as well as to the I.L.O. The task of the central office would be to stimulate the utilisation of the mass information media. The I.L.O. could, in this connection, help in the formation of such an organisation in those countries that asked for its assistance. In collaboration with other institutions, it could also undertake a study of the administrative, technical and financial aspects that are involved when recourse is had to mass information media for purposes of workers' education.

The most suitable types of programmes for broadcasting workers' education subjects using mass information media should be conceived in such a way as to bring about a fuller acquaintance with the basic problems of social and economic development. Among them would be various topics of current importance: how to study national and sub-regional economic integration or transformation of industries and economies, how to facilitate vocational training, how to enable workers to grasp the interplay of the basic factors which determine and shape their lives, such as population growth, technological progress, evolution and aspirations of the developing countries.

The list of subjects given below makes no claim to be exhaustive, and the character of the programmes, together with the relative importance that should be assigned to them, will naturally depend on local needs and requirements.

Programmes of an informational character

- Full and lively coverage of significant labour events.
- Interpretation of labour news.
- Interviews and discussions featuring outstanding labour leaders.
- Documentaries on important international, national, regional and local labour problems.
- Filmed reports on the labour movement designed for general audiences.
- Coverage of national or local labour campaigns.
- Labour's commentary and interpretation in connection with events, personalities and problems not exclusively related to labour questions.

Programmes of an educational character

- The history of labour (serial broadcasts).
- The need for trade unions, and their role in the improvement of living and working conditions (serial broadcasts).
- Improved effectiveness of trade unionists and their officers.
- Social and labour legislation.
- Industrial relations and communication within the enterprise (serial broadcasts).
- Industrial safety and hygiene.
- The role of women and youth within the labour force; social conditions of women; young workers, their work, life and the community.
- Social security.
- The working of the educational system especially in relation to the worker and his family.
- The full utilisation of leisure and of retirement.
- Population growth and its control.
- The effect of modern technology and automation on the everyday life of the workers, including such subjects as job evaluation, industrial engineering, etc.
- Introduction to basic economics including, for example: standard of living, national income determination and distribution; prices and wages and economic development, planning and integration.
- Vocational training.
- Problems of employment, including: unemployment, underemployment, labour mobility and redeployment.

Programmes of cultural character

- The promotion of understanding by the worker of his own culture.
- Dramatised presentations of a lively sort, concerning social themes.
- General culture, music, folklore and popular dances.
- Community education.

Regularly spaced programmes

As has been stated above, it is not feasible to leave it entirely up to the producers to decide on the nature of the programmes, their frequency and the way in which they are to be presented. At this point, close and permanent contacts should be maintained, involving technicians, producers, educators, trade unionists and public and private agencies interested in the question. As a result, we find a broad range is opened up for participation. Moreover, a collaboration of this sort cannot fail to simplify the task of the producer. In order to make the broadcasts really effective, it is vital that the radio audiences or the telespectators should be able to follow the programmes regularly, and this could not be ensured if the broadcasts aimed at the working public were to be put on sporadically, from time to time.

Production: means utilised

It does indeed seem clear that both television and radio ought to avoid falling back into any rigid and academic pattern of instruction. For that reason, film sequences, still photographs, slides, animated graphs, maps or diagrams are the most direct, and also the most economical tools for educational television, for example. The flannelboard, the flipchart, as well as the whole array of teaching devices developed in the audio-visual field could very well be used by producers and be adapted to the screen.

The experts felt that the television and radio programmes ought to be concrete and should present the facts in a lively manner, leaving it up to the radio audience and the telespectators to reach their own conclusions or, still better, providing them with the opportunity for a debate under the guidance of a group leader who would receive all the desired documentation as well as the scripts. It goes without saying that, while audience interest must be maintained, the concern to amuse and distract should not be pushed to the point of sacrificing the educational character of the broadcast, as happens all too often with broadcasts purporting to be educational.

Labour films could be far more effectively utilised than is now the case. The adoption of a proper svstem of indexing, classification and data retrieval could greatly facilitate this improved utilisation.

The group is still the best guarantee of effectiveness in teaching

The participants in the Workshop did not need to dwell at length on one fact that all educators have recognised, namely that teaching has little real impact on a passive audience. Therefore, when radio and television are used in workers' education, the effort should be made to bring about full participation of the workers in the "lesson", and it should be arranged to have the broadcasts followed by group discussions. Along these lines, the participants put forward, as something more specific, the possibility of presenting certain courses handled through the mass media, for example courses on vocational training or job safety, at the actual workplace and during normal working hours. This amounts to a supplementary aspect of educational leave, and thus a new area opened for collective bargaining.

Training

The systematic use of radio and television in labour education cannot be seriously contemplated without a special training effort involving not only the producers and technicians, but also the workers' educators.

The participants in the Workshop stressed the fact that the best way to ensure results in this respect would be for the radio and television agencies to recruit a number of producers having trade union backgrounds. At the same time, numbers of worker-educators should be given training in the special techniques of working with the radio and television networks. This could be taken care of by organising introductory courses for the trade union officers and instructors, and by familiarising trade union leaders with the fine points for doing well on the television screen: how to handle a debate or an interview, how best to express themselves for television, how to write scripts, etc.

Role of the I.L.O.

It is one of the tasks of the I.L.O., not only in the field of education, but in all the other fields within its scope, to give worldwide promotion to those advances in technology which its basic mission prompts it to recognise as contributing to the improvement of the workers' living conditions. Assistance lent to labour organisations for the development of their educational activities in social and economic respects therefore continues to occupy a leading place among its programmes. The need to work out more and more favourable conditions for the use of mass information media in the field of labour education has been stressed many times in the course of technical meetings convened by the I.L.O.

In collaboration with the U.N.E.S.C.O. and other interested institutions, the I.L.O. could envisage a number of interesting activities, which the Workshop participants listed as follows: drafting a manual on the utilisation of radio and television in labour education; assisting in the establishment of national co-ordinating machinery; setting up a system of exchange of information and documentation; publishing information and news, as well as giving accounts of experiences in the *Labour Education* Bulletin. Material produced by the various agencies broadcasting workers' education programmes over the radio and by television should be sent to the International Labour Office which, here again, would serve as a centre for documentation and distribution. Furthermore, the I.L.O. could be helpful in encouraging the production of teaching material such as films or film sequences. Workshop participants underscored the importance of having a study made on the possibilities of utilising mass information media for educational purposes. Such a study would deal with the following points: the needs, exploitation, organisation, utilisation, effectiveness and costs.

The participants in the Workshop expressed the hope that the I.L.O. could organise seminars or advisory missions, to bring about fuller practical collaboration between the worker educators and the broadcasting agencies. Fellowship grants could be allotted for training purposes. In this way, the worker educators would enrich their experiences and would be better equipped to contribute more fully to national, regional and international efforts in the field.

Lastly, the Workshop participants pointed out that the use of radio and television in workers' education is something that goes well beyond the interests of the producers and the workers' organisations. Many problems raised by such utilisation cannot be solved without the collaboration of governments as well as of employers, and for this reason the members of the Workshop suggested that this problem might become a subject for eventual discussion at some time in the near future, during a session of the International Labour Conference or within any other tripartite body of the I.L.O.

Robert Falaize

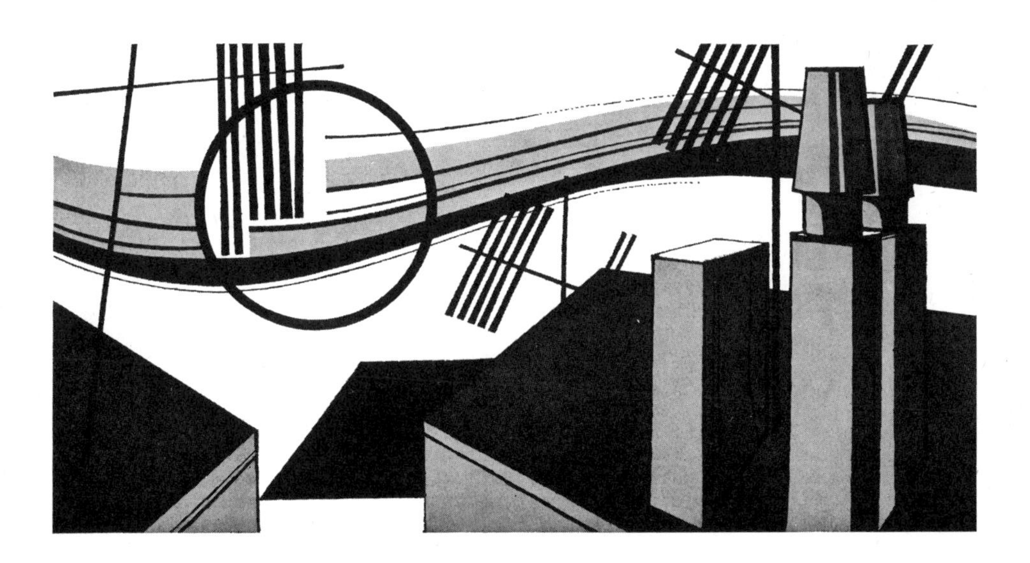

Representing the Union

A Series of Ten Programmes for Workers' Education Broadcast by the BBC

Anthony Matthews, the author of this article, is the producer of a television series on BBC which deserves great attention in workers' education – he himself explains why.

Mr. Matthews attended the ILO Workshop on the Use of Radio and Television for Workers' Education, held in Geneva in November 1967, in his capacity as television producer of social programmes on BBC[1]*. He is one of those Workshop participants who, upon returning home, thought seriously of putting into action some of the Workshop's findings and conclusions.*

•

The most publicised feature of the BBC television project "Representing the Union" was the fact that it caused at least one industrial dispute. In October 1969 shop stewards at a major engineering factory near London walked out of the works because the management would not permit them to watch the television programme during working hours. "Shop Stewards Walk Out to Watch TV" – this was the sort of headline that appeared in the national press next day.

The walk-out emphasised the unusual nature of the whole exercise. For the first time in Britain television broadcasting was being used as an instrument of shop steward education on a national scale. As a deliberate policy, the programmes were being transmitted during working hours to encourage the formation of viewing groups of stewards in factories and other workplaces.

This meant that the BBC series became a kind of catalytic agent in local industrial relations. Factory managements all over the country were approached by the unions to provide television viewing facilities and to release groups of shop stewards from work so that they could watch the series over a ten-week period. About 1,000 such groups were set up, and the evidence suggests that the majority of the viewing shop stewards did not lose any pay by meeting "in the boss's time". There are no figures for the number of viewing groups that were refused time off.

The background facts about the series itself are simple enough. It consisted of ten half-hour programmes broadcast in autumn 1969 on BBC-1. Each programme was transmitted on Sundays at 12.30 p.m. for viewers at home, and on Wednesdays at 3.45 p.m. for viewing groups in workplaces and colleges. (The series was repeated in autumn 1970 again with group use very much as the target.)

[1] See: *Labour Education*, No. 12, March 1968, page 27.

The programmes were accompanied by an impressive print package, consisting of five booklets and a set of guide notes for the man leading the viewing group.

The production of the series was preceded by about two years of discussion between the BBC and its educational advisers (including the TUC) on the question of what the objectives of the series should be and what audience it should be aimed at. Should it be a series about trade unions for the general public? Should it be a series about industrial relations, but aimed at a joint audience of managers as well as trade unionists? Or should it be aimed at a small minority audience of trade union representatives? These were tough questions, and each of the choices had strong advocates, both inside and outside the BBC.

In the event, a number of factors gave extra priority to the idea of a series for shop stewards. The first was the report of the Royal Commission on Trade Unions and Employers' Associations (the Donovan Report), which emphasised the key role of the shop steward in industry and the immense need for shop steward training. Over two-thirds of Britain's 175,000 shop stewards, said the Report, had received no training of any kind.

A second important factor that coloured our thoughts about the series was the rise of productivity bargaining in British industry during the late 1960's. Briefly, this trend, which was strengthened by the Government's incomes policy at the time, meant that a growing number of shop stewards were becoming involved in complex workplace bargaining. More and more managements, drawing in many cases on the services of management consultants, were coming to the negotiating table armed with package deals of pay and productivity proposals that were usually based on the use of modern management techniques. Shop steward negotiators were suddenly being faced with the complexities of work study, job evaluation and costing, in none of which had they received any previous training. In short, productivity bargaining was greatly increasing the pressures on the shop steward to be an efficient negotiator, communicator and representative.

Working closely with a small unit of advisers in the TUC's education department and consulting closely with major unions such as the Transport and General Workers and the Amalgamated Engineering Union, the production team found that the problems of productivity bargaining for the shop steward would be a useful and timely theme for the series. We made several visits to factories and trade union courses to meet shop stewards and to find out what their problems were. In all, we consulted eleven trade unions to get a fair consensus of opinion about the most useful things the series could do.

In the event, the series took about eight months to produce. During this period we organised preview conferences all over the country at which local employers and trade union representatives could see films of the programmes before they were broadcast. At the same time the TUC distributed 100,000 leaflets through the trade union network, giving details of the programmes and containing order forms for the vital package of booklets that went with the series. Without this kind of backing from the TUC, the series would not have been nearly as widely used as it was.

There were, however, some dangers in working so closely with the unions. Occasional rumblings were heard from employers that they were not being consulted and that the TUC and the BBC were conspiring to make life difficult for industrial management. There were even grumblings from the trade union world that the BBC was planning "to brainwash shop stewards on behalf of its friends, the employers". It was a project in which complete success was virtually impossible, and failure only too likely.

From the educational point of view, the most interesting feature of the whole television project was the use of the programmes and print material by viewing groups. A television set placed in the canteen, social club or training centre became the focal point of a group meeting which in many cases brought together shop stewards from different unions for the first time to discuss points of common interest which arose from the programme.

A group discussion followed each TV programme.

Having sat in with a number of viewing groups myself at the time, I have no doubt that it was the group discussion after the programme that was the most educationally valuable part of the exercise. This was confirmed by the shop stewards themselves, who said that the discussion afterwards helped them to appreciate and retain points in the programme better than if they had been viewing individually at home. The group discussion would also apply the general principles in the programme to the particular problems faced locally by the stewards. This was particularly useful to the newer shop stewards in the group, who were able to pick up tips and ideas from their more experienced colleagues. Some groups also contained managers and supervisors; indeed, in some cases where this was so, discussion sometimes turned into negotiation.

In linking this unusual combination of television, print and group discussion, the key figure was the group leader. In most cases he was not a trained tutor but a convenor or senior shop steward, with little or no experience of controlling an educational situation with the aid of television and print. We came across instances where the poor calibre of the group leader ruined the whole exercise. There were others where he rose magnificently to the occasion, but these were rare. In general, the effectiveness of the project was weakened by its dependence on untrained group leaders.

Nevertheless, the series and the tutor's notes both tried to help the novice group leader. The majority of the programmes were of the "straight teaching" variety. They used a combination of an illustrated talk on a management technique by an expert and critical response by a union commentator who pointed out a checklist of things the shop steward should watch out for if faced with the introduction of this technique. As a general rule, this sort of "straight" programme was appreciated by the inexperienced group leader more than the open-ended case-study programme which raised more questions than it answered. Significantly, professional group tutors preferred the latter type. Only two of the ten programmes were based on filmed case-studies of an actual problem.

The notes for tutors also assumed an inexperienced group leader. They contained instructions for organising and running the group, together with sections giving the precise aims and content of the programmes, points to watch for during the programme and questions for discussion after the programme. If points in the programmes were

A group of trade union representatives from a large printing firm near London.

obscure, the notes said so, and attempted to clarify them.

The design of the printed package – especially the study notes for tutors and students – required as much care as the design of the television programmes, if not more. Shop stewards are not great readers or writers, and our printed material may have expected too much of them in this respect They are, however, among the world's greatest talkers, so the real function of the study notes was to fuel the discussion after the programme and to relate it to the general principles outlined in the programme.

Sales of the BBC series booklet reached 26,000 copies, and 11,000 of the packages designed for group use were sold, largely in response to orders resulting from the TUC's distribution of 100,000 leaflets/order forms. Most of these orders flowed in during the last few weeks before the series started. A severe bottleneck was caused here. The programmes were not finally recorded until about a month before transmission, and this meant that the vital study notes had to be completed at such a late stage that distribution of the packages was badly delayed. In the event, thanks to a hardworked BBC publication staff, most of the parcels of booklets did get to customers on time.

Towards the tail-end of the series, the Commission on Industrial Relations carried out some research into the effectiveness of the project. About 800 groups of people were contacted who had either formed viewing groups or stated their intention to do so when they ordered the series booklets. The following are some of the salient facts that have come from a preliminary analysis:

1. Shop stewards were asked how willing they would be to recommend the repeat of the series to other shop stewards. The following table summarises the replies:

Very willing	61 per cent of sample
Quite willing.....	31 ,, ,, ,, ,,
Slightly willing ...	5 ,, ,, ,, ,,
Not willing	3 ,, ,, ,, ,,

2. Shop stewards were asked how useful the series was in giving them an idea of the problems involved in productivity bargaining. The following table summarises the replies:

Very useful	46 per cent of sample
Quite useful	44 ,, ,, ,, ,,
Slightly useful....	9 ,, ,, ,, ,,
Not useful.......	1 ,, ,, ,, ,,

3. Group leaders were asked how useful the programmes were to them as an educational aid. The following table summarises the replies:

Very useful	45 per cent of sample
Quite useful	42 „ „ „ „
Slightly useful....	11 „ „ „ „
Not useful.......	2 „ „ „ „

4. Group leaders were asked how much of the viewing group's meeting time was spent during working hours:

   68 per cent of sample spent *all* of meeting time during working hours;

   23 per cent of sample spent *some* of meeting time during working hours.

5. Group leaders were asked whether the viewing group's meetings were held on company premises:

   76 per cent of the sample said meetings were held on company premises;

   of those whose meetings were *not* held on company premises approximately 40 per cent were held in an educational establishment.

(This research project was undertaken by E. E. Coker and W. M. Conboy, Staff Tutors in Industrial Relations at Oxford University, Rowley House, Wellington Square.)

We have aimed throughout the project to give "Representing the Union" a useful life beyond the repeat broadcast in the autumn of 1970. Seven of the original ten programmes are now available for sale or hire as 16 mm films, through BBC Television Enterprises. During the next five years they will be on offer as visual aids for use in any formal course of shop steward education. They have the great advantage of being the only films made exclusively for this purpose.

Aims of the Programmes

Programme 1:

"What is Productivity Bargaining?"

To introduce the subject by setting out an example of a productivity bargain; to discuss the dangers and pitfalls and to assess some of the opportunities of productivity bargaining for both workers and management.

To provide the basis for discussion on the nature and importance of productivity bargaining.

Programme 2:

"Negotiating the Bargain"

To demonstrate some of the problems of communications involved in negotiating a productivity bargain.

To explore methods of improving communications.

To provide the basis for discussion on their improvement.

Programme 3:

"Communicating with the Members"

To illustrate the process of reporting to the members a proposed wage agreement involving some productivity elements; and then bringing the members together to accept the proposals.

To comment on the effectiveness of the communications and to discuss the various means used.

To form the basis for a discussion on the method of effective communications with the members.

Programme 4:

"Costs and the Pay Packet"

To consider why shop stewards should understand costing.

To demonstrate the principles behind cost accounting.

To provide the basis for a discussion about the importance of costing in productivity bargaining.

Programme 5:

"A Fair Differential"

To consider the origin and function of differential rates of payment in industry.

To discuss the problems which arise from unsatisfactory differentials.

To suggest means of relating rates of payment to job structures.

To provide the basis of a discussion on the importance of differentials in productivity bargaining.

Programme 6:

"The New Pay Structure"

To explain the purpose behind job evaluation.

To analyse the method involved in job evaluation.

To provide the basis for discussions on the effectiveness of job evaluation as a basis for building a pay structure.

Programme 7:

"Measuring Work"

To discuss the purpose of work study.

To demonstrate some of the procedure in measuring work.

To provide the basis for a discussion on the shop steward's responsibilities when faced with work study.

Programme 8:

"Measuring Work for Non-Manual Employees"

To examine to what extent work measurement is applicable to non-manual (or indirect) workers.

To discuss, in very general terms, some of the methods used in such measurement; and to determine trade union attitudes to it.

Programme 9:

"A Fair Day's Pay"

To explain how systems of payment by results operate.

To assess the motives of management in introducing them.

To investigate trade union attitudes to payment by results; and to provide the basis for a discussion about the methods and effects of payment by results.

Programme 10:

"The Future of Productivity Bargaining"

To consider what are likely to be the major developments in productivity bargaining.

To assess what will be their implications for management and trade unions; and to provide the basis for a discussion on shop stewards' responsibilities in this field.

Anthony Matthews

Filming a shop floor discussion which was watched all over the country.

Jean-Marie ALBERTINI

A New Teaching Aid for Basic Economics: The Game of Ecoplany

Ecoplany *is the brain-child of Mr. J.-M. Albertini who is in charge of research at the French National Scientific Research Centre and a member of the* Economy and Humanism *group. It is published in Paris by Editions Ouvrières, and has been approved by the National Pedagogical Institute. In this article, the inventor introduces* Ecoplany *and explains its importance in the teaching of basic economics.*

•

Our aim in devising the game of Ecoplany **was to introduce basic economics and to provide an understanding of economic processes by avoiding some of the disadvantages of more traditional methods such as books, lectures or discussion groups. However, we do not claim to have discovered a miracle teaching aid. It goes without saying that the role of** Ecoplany **must be limited and clearly defined. It is not possible to understand fully the significance of this game unless it is considered in the context of the method that we are trying to perfect. Therefore, I propose to start by giving a brief description of the rules of the game and then I shall describe, firstly, the pedagogical principles behind our method for teaching basic economics and, secondly, the possible uses to which** Ecoplany **can be put.**

Ecoplany? What is it?

Ecoplany is, so to speak, a cross between the French family game known as "goose" and national accounting[1].

Of what does it consist?

Each player – or team of players – has to manage an economy which is represented by a large card on which are portrayed, in simplified form,

[1] *"A game played with two dice on a board on which are depicted geese, set out in squares, nine by nine" (Petit Larousse – p. 718 – Oie). It is similar to the game "Luds" played in certain other countries.*

the resources which make up the nation's assets and the uses to which these assets may be put.

We should remember that the resources which constitute a nation's assets are the goods and services of which the economy disposes. These are either produced or imported. The uses to which these assets are put are those to which resources are usually put (household consumption, civil and military authorities' purchases, capital investment, housing, public services, exports). The resources and the uses must inevitably be equal, as the latter are in effect simply the resources classified according to use.

At the beginning of the game, each player – or team of players – receives from the Bank:

- 610,000 million in chips which he places on the available resources table in accordance with the instructions written on that table,
- 610,000 million in chips which he places on the uses table according to the instructions given by the "starting credits" on that table.

The game starts with all players in the same situation.

Apart from the above, each player – or team of players – receives 30,000 million in foreign currency notes with which to pay any possible foreign trade deficit.

The players sit round a large board on which are marked the various ups and downs which may occur in the running of an economy. This is where *Ecoplany* resembles "goose". The economic possibilities are set out in forty squares which form a track around the board and which represent fortunate or unfortunate events such as growth of investments, increased consumption, strikes, inflation, increased productivity, leakage of capital and an increased available labour force.

At the beginning of the game, each player – or group of players – puts the counter representing his – or their – economy in the square "go". He then moves round the track by rolling the dice and advancing as many squares as the dice indicate.

How the game is played

Each of the economic events, as shown in the squares, causes an imbalance in the table of resources and uses. Since the player is obliged to keep the resources and uses in perfect balance he may, when production improves, increase the uses. If production drops he may either reduce the uses or increase imports. If one of the uses has to be increased without a corresponding rise in production, then the player may either increase imports or cut back on other uses, transferring the extra resources thus obtained to the use which requires increasing.

Let us imagine that starting from the square "go", a player throws the dice for 6. He would therefore move his counter to square 6. The instructions given in this square read as follows:

> *Your successful training policy has enabled you to increase the productivity of your undertaking; your production increases by 30,000 million if your capital investments are at least 70,000 million.*

What happens next?

1. A count is made to ensure that the player does in fact have 70,000 million of capital investments. Because we are assuming that this is the first throw of the game, he does in fact have the required sum, as the starting credit for capital investments is 70,000 million.
2. The player receives 60,000 million worth of chips, half of which he must place on the item "production" on his card, as this is the first instruction in square 6. He is left with 30,000 million to increase his uses.

He may distribute this sum as he sees fit. He may, for example, choose to make purchases for the military authorities if he is in favour of armament, or he may put it into capital investment if he wants to build up reserves, or into household consumption if he is in favour of the immediate satisfaction of the consumer; he may invest in public property if he wants to take a stand against the consumer society, or, yet again, in exports if he wishes to conquer foreign markets ... or he may combine several of these possibilities.

The choices thus reflect the various options open to the players

However, the player cannot ignore the dictates of the economy. The first of these is obviously the demands of the market, i.e. resources must be found to meet increased uses. The second, imposed by the rules of the game, are the consequences of past activity or of previous choices. In fact, the player can only modify his uses in accordance with the instructions given in the squares on which he lands and his choice of action will influence the rest of the game.

If he ignores household consumption, while the other sectors of the economy prosper, he is likely to be faced with a general strike (square 10). If he neglects capital investment he will not, on a later occasion, be able to set up production to take advantage of favourable events. If he does not increase exports and if he increases imports to avoid a drop in certain uses, he will have to pay off his deficit in foreign currency units when he next passes "go". If he has the misfortune to land on square 30, he may have to devalue his currency and be prepared for austerity measures. If he neglects housing he may have trouble catching up again. And so on. The economic events are arranged around the board in accordance with a plan which will force the players to understand the consequence of their choices, the mechanisms of the economy and the relations between over-all economic choices and economic forces. In this, *Ecoplany* adheres closely to the criteria which we have tried to respect in preparing our method for the teaching of economics.

To what method of teaching does *Ecoplany* subscribe?

Our pedagogical research is aimed mainly at the less well informed members of the public and is limited to an introduction, but an introduction to the economy does not consist simply of a transfer of knowledge. The economy is above all the expression of a social process. There are undoubtedly constants and variable forces, but these elements are themselves connected with the activities of different groups, with patterns of behaviour and with choices. An introduction to the economy therefore requires a better insight into the social process which is at the very root of the economy, so that more effective action may be achieved through an improved understanding of the process. Teaching methods must not, therefore, seek to modify the way in which the economy in fact works – for example, by changing the motivation of an individual or of a group to the advantage of another group. Rather, they should make it easier for the student to master the information, to exercise judgment and to attain greater freedom of thought as distinct from the bare accumulation of facts. Hence the introduction, in addition to providing the minimum necessary for communication and discussion, should aim at action and not just a transfer of knowledge.

Starting from this point and drawing on past experience, we believe that until such time as more precise information can be obtained three criteria should be applied to the teaching of basic economics:

- the criterion of the over-all approach,
- the criterion of the concrete approach,
- the criterion of the practical approach.

Ecoplany tries, in so far as is possible, to follow these three criteria.

The criterion of the over-all approach

In teaching people a social practice and increasing their capacity for judgment, it may be assumed that the starting point will be an over-all view of the subject, because it is necessary first of all to show the relations between the various elements of the economy. For this reason, business economics or even family economics must take second place. Naturally, the over-all approach does not mean that we should not consider the practical and every-day problems of the environment in which we live; rather that, to start with, the horizon should be as broad as possible. It is when we get beyond this horizon that individual problems will take on their true meaning. This approach is found both in our publications[1] and the schemes which they contain and in *Ecoplany*. It is not a coincidence that we started by divising a game which puts the players in con-

[1] Les rouages de l'économie nationale, *1960 (The Wheels of the National Economy);* Les Premiers Pas en Economie, *1969 (First Steps in Economics);* Les Mécanismes du sous-développement, *1967 (The Mechanics of Under-Development), published by Editions Ouvrières – Economie et Humanisme, Paris.*

ECOPLANY
Une réalisation de J.-M. Albertini
ECOPLANY
Une réalisation de J.-M. Albertini
Les accidents de parcours de l'Economie Nationale
DEPART
Au passage payez en devises le montant de votre déficit commercial ou recevez en devises le montant de votre excédent commercial. Dans ce cas vous pouvez importer pour 10 milliards.
Des jeunes plus nombreux arrivent à l'âge du travail. Votre production augmente de 30 milliards, si vos investissements productifs s'élèvent au moins à 70 milliards. ALLEZ EN 29
Vous devez lutter contre la crise du logement. Si vos dépenses de logements sont inférieures à 40 milliards, vous devez les porter à 60 milliards.
Les banques orientent le crédit vers les investissements productifs qui augmentent de 20 milliards. ALLEZ EN 31.
Les salaires augmentent. La consommation s'accroît de 30 milliards. ALLEZ si impair : EN 12. si pair : EN 13.
Si un seul des partenaires a une plus petite production que les autres, ses entrepreneurs préfèrent investir dans votre économie plutôt que dans la sienne. Il perd à votre profit 10 milliards d'investissements, 10 milliards de devises et 10 milliards
Votre politique de formation vous permet d'accroître la productivité de vos entreprises. Votre production s'accroît de 30 milliards si vos investissements productifs s'élèvent au moins à 70 milliards.
Il y a bientôt des élections. Vous faites construire des piscines et créer de nouvelles autoroutes. Vos équipements collectifs augmentent de 10 milliards. ALLEZ si impair : EN 11. si pair : EN 11.
La guerre menace. Si vous n'avez pas d'achats des administrations militaires, vous devez en faire pour 20 milliards, et ne pas les réduire avant d'avoir effectué un tour de circuit.
L'immigration de travailleurs étrangers vous permet d'accroître la production de 20 milliards, si vos investissements productifs sont égaux ou supérieurs à 50 milliards.
Si vous avez l'une des plus petites consomm des ménages, par suite de politique sociale, il y a grève générale. Vous laissez passer un Vous perdez 70 milliar production.
11 Vous n'avez pas de capacité de production inutilisée. Pour faire face aux dépenses d'équipements collectifs, vous devez réduire les autres emplois ou accroître les importations de 10 milliards pour augmenter d'autant les équipements collectifs.
12 L'accroissement de la consommation stimule une expansion de 40 milliards de la production dont la capacité était en partie inutilisée.
13 Vous n'avez pas de capacité de production inutilisée pour faire face à l'accroissement de la consommation. Vous devez réduire les autres emplois ou accroître les importations de 30 milliards pour augmenter d'autant la consommation.
14 L'accroissement des dépenses d'équipements collectifs provoque une expansion de 30 milliards de la production dont la capacité n'était pas pleinement utilisée.
15 Si vous n'avez pas la plus grande production et que l'un de vos partenaires ait une plus grande production que les autres, vos entrepreneurs préfèrent investir dans son économie plutôt que dans la vôtre. Vous perdez à son profit 10 milliards d'investissement productif, 10 milliards de production et 10 milliards de devises.
16 Si vous avez la plus grande consommation, pour faire face à l'accroissement de la demande et lutter contre la hausse des prix le gouvernement facilite les importations qui augmentent de 20 milliards.
17 Vos prix augmentent plus rapidement que les prix étrangers. Vos exportations diminuent de 20 milliards, Vos importations augmentent de 20 milliards. Si impair : ALLEZ EN 37.
18 Vos entrepreneurs deviennent plus compétents et dynamiques. Votre production s'accroît de 30 milliards si vous avez un minimum de 80 milliards d'investissements productifs.
19 Les placements improductifs (comme la spéculation foncière et la thésaurisation en or) diminuent. Vos investissements productifs augmentent de 10 milliards et votre production de 40 milliards.
20 Si vous êtes seul à avoir les plus grands achats des administrations militaires ou les plus petits, vous êtes entraîné à la guerre. Vous laissez passer un tour, vous augmentez de 40 milliards vos achats de matériel militaire, votre production diminue de 70 milliards.
21 L'expansion dans les autres pays se propage dans votre économie. Vos exportations augmentent de 20 milliards et votre production de 40 milliards, car votre capacité de production n'était pas pleinement utilisée.
22 Davantage de femmes travaillent. Votre production augmente de 20 milliards. ALLEZ EN 29.
23 Pour lutter contre l'inflation, vous diminuez les dépenses budgétaires en réduisant de 20 milliards au total : · Achats des administrations civiles. · Achats de matériel militaire. · Equipements collectifs pour augmenter la consommation. si impair : ALLEZ EN 33.
24 Si vous avez moins de 90 milliards d'investissements productifs : vos banques n'orientent pas suffisamment leurs crédits vers les investissements productifs qui diminuent de 20 milliards. La consommation profite de cette diminution et augmente de 20 milliards. ALLEZ EN 38.
25 Les mauvaises récoltes entraînent une baisse de 30 milliards de la production agricole. Vos exportations diminuent de 20 milliards. Si impair : ALLEZ EN 30.
26 Par suite d'une hausse des prix plus rapide qu'à l'étranger, il y a une spéculation contre votre monnaie. Vous perdez 30 milliards de devises. Si vous ne les avez pas, vous devez les emprunter. ALLEZ EN 30.
27 Les salariés obtiennent une réduction de la durée du travail avec maintien des salaires. Au lieu de faire 45 h de travail par semaine en moyenne, ils n'en feront que 40. La production chute de 30 milliards. si impair : ALLEZ EN 28.
28 L'efficacité de vos services de recherche vous permet de mettre au point des méthodes de production nouvelles. Votre production s'accroît de 50 milliards si vos investissements productifs atteignent 80 milliards et vos importations 110 milliards.
29 Si vos équipements collectifs sont inférieurs à 20 milliards, vous devez les porter à 40 milliards pour faire face notamment à la montée des jeunes et à l'accroissement du travail féminin.
30 Si vous avez un déficit du commerce extérieur, vous êtes obligé de dévaluer. Vos exportations augmentent de 30 milliards et vos importations diminuent de 30 milliards. Tous les autres partenaires doivent diminuer leurs exportations de 10 milliards et leur production chute de 20 milliards.
31 Grâce à votre politique d'investissements votre production s'accroît de 50 milliards si vos investissements productifs atteignent 90 milliards et vos importations 110 milliards.
32 Pour lutter contre l'inflation, vous diminuez les crédits aux entreprises. Vos investissements productifs diminuent de 20 milliards au profit des emplois. ALLEZ EN 34.
33 Vos économies budgétaires provoquent une chute de la demande. La crise qui s'ensuit aboutit à une diminution de 30 milliards de la consommation des ménages.
34 Si vous avez les plus petits investissements productifs : La diminution des investissements productifs provoque une crise dans les industries d'équipements. La consommation des ménages diminue de 30 milliards.
35 Une planification efficace facilite la croissance de votre production, qui augmente de 60 milliards. Mais, pour réaliser une telle croissance, vous devez avoir 90 milliards d'investissements productifs et 120 milliards d'importations.
36 Pour lutter contre l'inflation vous devez restreindre le crédit à la consommation. La consommation diminue de 30 milliards dont bénéficient les emplois de votre choix.
37 Si vous n'avez pas un excédent du commerce extérieur, l'accroissement des importations et la diminution de vos exportations provoquent une crise. La production diminue de 40 milliards.
38 Si vous avez moins de 70 milliards d'investissements, votre politique d'investissement est insuffisante. Durant un tour de circuit vous n'avez pas le droit d'accroître la production.
39 L'exode rural s'amplifie. Vous disposez de plus de main-d'oeuvre industrielle, votre production s'accroît de 30 milliards. Mais la crise du logement s'accentue. ALLEZ EN 2.
© Editions ouvrières 1969 Marque et modèle déposés E.O. E.H. n° 2625

A selection of squares from the Ecoplany board

7

Election time is coming up. You build swimming pools and new motorways.

Your public property increases by 10 thousand million.

if you roll an even number:
Go to 11

if you roll an odd number:
Go to 14

11

You have no unused production capacity. To cover public property expenditures, you have to reduce other expenses or increase imports by 10 thousand million to increase public property by as much.

14

The increase in public property expenditures causes a 30 thousand million franc expansion in production capacity which was not fully utilised until now.

23

To combat inflation, you curtail budgetary expenses by an over-all 20 thousand million franc reduction in:

- public administration expenses
- military equipment expenses
- public property to increase consumption.

if you roll an odd number:
Go to 33

26

As a result of a more rapid rise in prices than in foreign countries there is speculation on your currency.

You lose 30 thousand million in foreign currency. If you have not got that much, you have to borrow it.

Go to 30

30

If you have a foreign trade deficit, you have to devalue.

Your exports increase by 30 thousand million and your imports decrease by 30 thousand million.

Your partners have to reduce their exports by 10 thousand million and their production falls by 20 thousand million.

33

Your budgetary savings cause a decrease in demand. The ensuing crisis leads to a 30 thousand million franc decrease in household consumption.

35

Efficacious planning makes possible the intensification of your production, which expands by 60 thousand million. However, in order to bring about such an increase, you have to have 90 thousand million francs in productive investments and 120 thousand million in imports.

trol of a national economy and not of a business or family economy.

However, this approach has one disadvantage. By trying to broaden the horizon we run the risk of alienating the interest of the person studying the introduction. This danger is far from insignificant as the *Ecoplany* board presents the economy in an abstract manner bearing no relation to the individual's experience and motivation.

The criterion of the concrete approach

In fact, it should never be forgotten that the economy consists of every-day life, and that, possibly without being aware of it, each and every one of us makes the economy and that it dominates our cultural environment. Economic news

is constantly being disseminated and many conversations at the work place, at the hairdresser's or at home in the evening often turn on most significant issues. Most of our contemporaries are really economic illiterates. They know a language but they have never been taught how to read or write it. They have simply not mastered it. As in the case of true illiterates, their behaviour is influenced by false ideas and self-propagating myths.

If we really want to give an introduction to basic economics, we must start with facts and information with which the pupils are already acquainted or of which they have some idea. We must induce them to observe and compare such information. In our method, when teaching basic principles, we have laid particular stress on programmed teaching, which makes it possible for the pupil to master the items of information and gradually piece them together. In the case of the game of *Ecoplany* our starting point was economic policy and action, to which I have referred. The board on which the track is set out is accompanied by a leaflet which enables the students to comment on each case in the light of actual economic problems.

It is, therefore, not by chance that the economy on which the game is based is essentially concrete and particular, and that the stress is laid on policy problems and not on economic theory. The latter is useful for specialists, but it belongs to a later stage of education, not to the introduction. At the level with which we are dealing, the introduction to basic economics must start from a description of known facts and, given the need for analysis and decision imposed by *Ecoplany*, of facts which make the players feel personally involved and which lead to that practical approach which constitutes our third criterion.

The criterion of the practical approach

The criterion of the practical approach is necessary if we wish not merely to set out from already acquired knowledge, but to understand truly what the economy really means. Nothing could be more dangerous than to make it appear a mechanical process. It is of the utmost importance to understand that while economic forces do exist, the economy is shaped by the choices of various social and economic groups and their interaction. From this point of view, the method

TABLE OF RESOURCES AND USES IN THE FIFTH FRENCH ECONOMIC PLAN – 1970

(in thousands of millions of francs)

Resources	*Uses*	
Production 462,55	Household consumption	314,50
Imports 78,84	Consumption (buying) by – public administrations – military administrations	 10 13,48
	Consumption by financial institutions (banks)	2,37
	Productive investments	67,42
	Housing construction	28,55
	Administrative investments (public property)	16,73
	Investments of financial institutions	0,53
	Variations in reserves	7,07
	Exports	80,74
Total 541,39		541,39

of these games is particularly interesting and effectively supplements programmed teaching. This is not to say that small discussion groups which are not faced with practical policy making or associated decisions can never be of use. The fact nevertheless remains that, given the economic misconceptions and superstitions of the majority of people, such groups often get bogged down in trifling discussions or fall into vague, theoretical policy setting unrelated to reality or into mere declamation. We prefer the method of involving or associating the student through the technique of the instructional game.

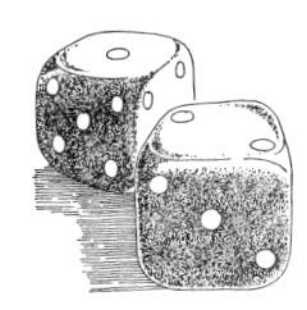

In this associative method, the participants are helped, by means of an interplay of question and answer, to bring to the surface existing relationships and to criticise them.

The technique of the game obliges each participant to play a role, to commit himself, to make a choice and to oppose the other players. Discussions arise as a matter of course. The outlines of some such games are very flexible. The first game that we prepared, for example, called *Ecocircuit,* was one in which the players represent various economic agents (households, undertakings, economic authorities and institutions). By means of some preliminary sequences they reconstitute the various relations between the economic agents and analyse the situations to which they lead. *Ecoplany* is a more strictly defined game and can therefore be more widely distributed. It might almost be compared with a business game but it does not call for the services of a computer. From a pedagogical point of view, this simplicity is not a disadvantage, for, at this introductory level, the use of a computer would probably restrict distribution and would also entail some genuine handicaps. Choice by computer would tend to accentuate the mysterious character of the economy instead of sweeping it away.

That said, we should never lose sight of the fact that a pedagogical game is still a simplification, a type of case study of which we are merely given the outlines and which requires very clear cut attitudes. This simplification is only a teaching aid, the grounds for discussion or for more detailed explanations. The way in which it is used is just as important as its content.

How is Ecoplany to be used?

Ecoplany may first of all be used as a simple party game. It gives a feeling for basic balances and forces, an understanding of certain choices and it familiarises the players with a vocabulary. The questionnaire which we put out to players and organisations using the game, and to which we received some 300 answers, showed that young children, 10 to 12 year olds, find it interesting. In their case the pedagogical value is limited, for children never advance beyond the stage of a game. They do, however, pick up a vocabulary and, if their parents play with them, this may spark off a discussion. This is particularly so when it comes to deciding which use to sacrifice when a choice has to be made between divergent interests. In this way it is possible to pass from the vocabulary to the political problems.

Among adults, *Ecoplany* gives rise to animated discussions and often serves not only as a perfect method of testing the players' knowledge but also of discovering the political opinions of one's friends. For those who wish to take it beyond the game stage, the card bearing economic observations on each of the squares may serve as a first introduction to the economy or, at least, to the problems raised in the game.

The use of *Ecoplany,* as a party game is, of course, only a secondary use. We aimed, above all, to create an aid for the teaching of general basic economics.

Normally, it is not introduced until after the cycle of the national economy has been explained and the basic elements of the economy have been analysed. Therefore, when I am in charge of a course on basic economics, I carry out the first stage, using the associative method, by showing

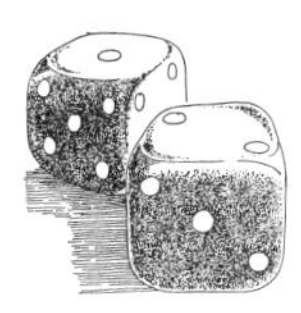

how the economic cycle is made up (by means of a model which breaks down) and the game of *Ecocircuit,* which I mentioned above. As soon as possible this is supplemented by readings from the book on the programmed method *Premiers pas en économie* (First Steps in Economics) or the textbook *Les rouages de l'économie nationale* (The Wheels of the National Economy). *Ecoplany* is used to introduce the movements of the economy (expansion, growth, inflation, recession, exports) and economic politics. This is then followed by sessions during which long and short term economic policies leading to the basic problems of modern society are explained.

Ecoplany is only, therefore, a stage in basic economic training.

We would suggest that the players be divided into teams, the members of which represent the government and social groups such as trade unions or employers. In this way, the group's choice will be the result of an interplay of different interests and political concepts.

As the game progresses, further explanations are given. The game leader may, at the beginning, use the leaflet of economic observations to explain the meaning of the squares. At the start of the game the explanations can be very basic, becoming progressively more complicated as a team's counter lands on a certain square. At the end, the play of each of the teams is discussed. In the early stages, the observations deal only with the forces (shortages, need to invest to boost production, need to increase consumption in line with production). Then stress can be laid on the different possible choices and the opposing interests within the given team. Once the players have acquired sufficient knowledge, they may be asked what measures would enable them to balance the resources and uses which they choose (budget expenditure, taxation, raising of tariff barriers, credit adjustments). As the players' knowledge broadens further, the game leader can ask for more precise observations. The first games played are devoted to the game itself and the assimilation of facts, while later games are used to analyse economic and social aspects.

At the end of a game, the players may be called upon to compare the percentage breakdown of uses with which each team has been left and the breakdown of uses in the countries of the players. At this stage we get on to a more directly political explanation. The discussion can also deal with the way in which the economy grows, its significance and the economic, political and social problems created by moving from one method of growth to another.

It can be seen that the use of *Ecoplany* can be very flexible and varied. At present we are trying to define its various applications and to prepare a guide on this subject. This research is part of a broader methodology. In fact, starting with an analysis of the cost factor and the drawing up of a technique of evaluation, we shall go on to decide upon the possible roles of the various teaching methods and aids. There is no miracle method or technique. The combination of the different teaching techniques must vary in accordance with the type of student and the level of instruction. In fact, we are now only just breaking new ground in this respect. The main thing is not to forget the object of teaching methods and aids is not to put over a message but to enable the greatest possible number of individuals to step into positions of responsibility in the economic, social and political fields.

SETTLE or STRIKE

Learning by playing:
A union-management collective bargaining simulation exercise

In issue No. 19 (June 1970) of *Labour Education* we introduced the game of **Ecoplany,** a teaching aid for basic economics created by Jean-Marie Albertini.

In this issue we would like to describe another game called **Settle or Strike** and how it can be used in teaching about labour relations. **Settle or Strike** was developed in 1967 as a part of the Communication Workers of America (CWA) Materials Project in co-operation with the School for Workers of the University of Wisconsin and Local 5530 of the CWA. It was prepared by Ray Glazier and Martha Rosen of ABT Associates of Cambridge, Massachusetts, in consultation with Irving Rosenstein of the Philadelphia Public Schools and the CWA Education Department.

What is "Settle or Strike"?

Settle or Strike is a teaching method that combines the ancient technique of gaming with the relatively recent technique of simulation.

Simulation may be explained as an exercise that permits the student to place himself in a structured role and to learn by experiencing the problems and feelings of another person. It could also be described as a kind of role-playing.

As a result of the active participation and involvement of the student while he is playing **Settle or Strike,** self-directed learning occurs, usually in three, successive, phases:

- learning the facts expressed in the game context and dynamics;
- learning the processes simulated by the game; and
- learning the relative costs and benefits, risks and potential rewards of alternative strategies of decision making.

The main purpose of **Settle or Strike** is to give the players an idea of the functioning of labour relations and, in particular, collective bargaining procedures. The game is not intended to "teach bargaining", but to expose the players to various types of information important in successful collective bargaining, to practical problems that arise at the bargaining table and to the strategic problems confronting both parties engaged in collective bargaining as a means of achieving peaceful labour relations. The game may also teach the players ways of securing the kinds of information required to present convincing, effective arguments to the opposing team.

The game highlights such problems as:

- preparation for negotiation;
- pricing of proposals;
- labour law;
- national policy implications in bargaining;
- information to union membership and the community during bargaining;
- factors outside the bargaining room that affect the settlement.

A variety of specific bargaining situations – multi-plant bargaining, government-employee bargaining, multi-union bargaining or multi-employer bargaining, for example – may be represented by **Settle or Strike.**

It is also flexible in the way it can be used. Union representatives, management-labour relations personnel, executives and government officials who need to understand the nature of labour relations will find it a valuable teaching aid. It may be used for union education and staff training, business management classes, university classes in economics, sociology, psychology and other social sciences, vocational and business education curricula, pre-apprenticeship and apprenticeship programmes and other programmes in which an understanding of collective bargaining is important.

How the game is played

Setting. – *The setting for* **Settle or Strike** *is Rapids Junction, a small town (pop. 8,620) in the midwestern United States. The Lastik Plastic Company is one of nine factories in the town. There are three unions in Rapids Junction: the Paper Makers Union, the Carpenters Union and the recently organised CWA unit at Lastik Plastik. This unit is a part of Local 0001, covering bargaining units in several towns.*

Lastik Plastik opened twelve years ago. Only a few of its employees have been with the company since its beginning. The production manager has been with the company for eleven years.

In October of last year several employees of Lastik Plastik contacted the President of CWA Local 0001 about organising a trade union in the plant. Their basic complaint was low wages, but they also felt that bringing in a union would help the employees obtain better working conditions. Local 0001 helped the employees organise and obtained certification as the bargaining agent. In February an election was held to elect a chairman of the Lastik Plastik unit of Local 0001. The sixty-day notice requirement was filed in March and the company and the union teams are now about to sit down and begin negotiations.

Settle or Strike can be played by an instructor and six players, three on the management team and three on the union team:

Management Lastik Plastik Company	**Union CWA**
• Company President	• President, CWA Local 0001
• Company Lawyer-Accountant	• Chairman, Lastik Plastik Unit
• Production Manager	• Staff Representative

The team spokesman has the most important role on each team. On the company team, this is the lawyer, and on the union team, the president of the CWA Local. The responsibility of the team spokesman is to present his team's position to the other side in clear, effective terms.

At the beginning of the game, each player receives a folder containing (1) *a role profile*, which is the description of the role he is to play and his personal position on the various bargaining issues; (2) a Rapids Junction *scenario* with information on the town, a historical summary of the formation of the Lastik Plastik Unit of CWA Local 0001, a summary of union demands and a description of the labour market situation in Rapids Junction; (3) *a team profile* describing each team's current position on the five issues to be negotiated during the game.

The game requires a maximum of six hours to play. This includes time for a review of the game rules, three team caucus sessions, each followed by three negotiating sessions, and a discussion of the results and experience at the end of the game. The caucus sessions provide the players on each team with time to plan their strategy for the negotiating sessions. They must prepare their proposals on all five issues and economic justification for these proposals, and they must also determine what range of alternatives they will be willing to accept from the other side. During the negotiating sessions they will make trade-offs and concessions in an attempt to reach a settlement.

The bargaining procedure will be centred on the following five issues: wages, union

security, vacations, seniority and contact length. For each issue, there are six possible positions. On wages, for example, there are possible increases of 50 cents, 40 cents, 30 cents, 20 cents, 10 cents per hour, or no increase at all. On each issue, the first alternative given is most favourable to the union and the sixth alternative is most favourable to the company.

The objective of the union team is to obtain an agreement from the company which incorporates as many of the membership's demands as possible, so that the agreement will be ratified by the rank and file.

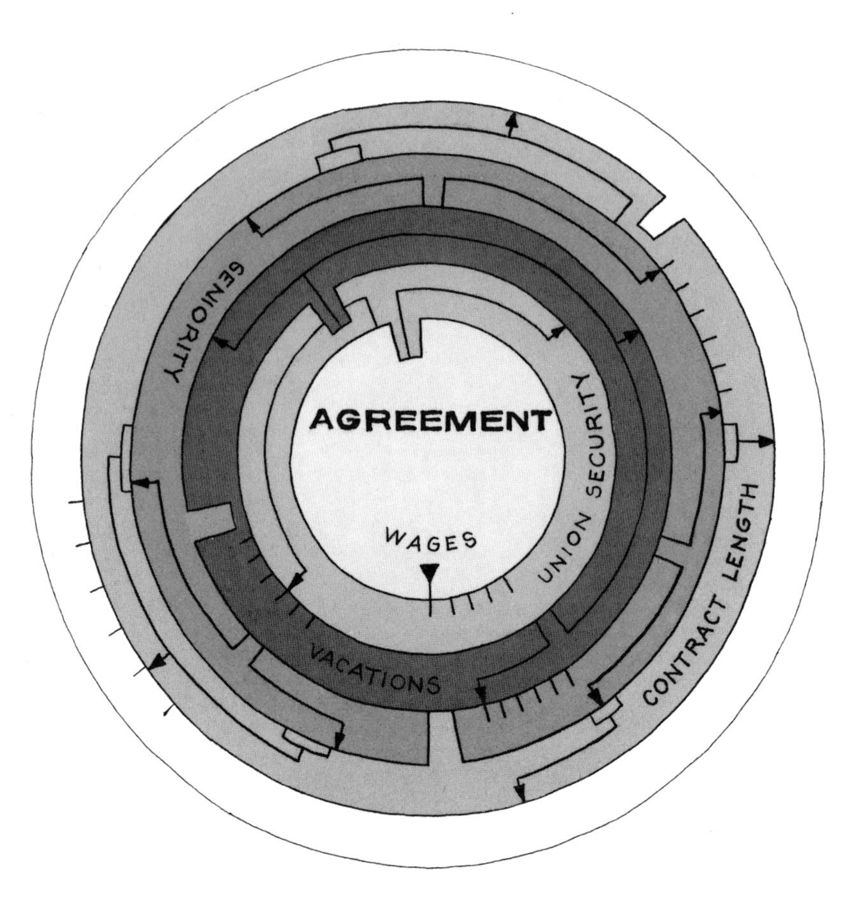

The objective of the company team is to achieve an agreement with the union that will allow management to retain as much operating flexibility as possible, and which is least costly.

Agreement Result Calculator

At the end of the game the positions of the teams are evaluated according to the way they settled or according to the amount by which they are separated by non-agreement. These values are fed into an Agreement Result Calculator (ARC), which then gives one of twenty-one possible results.

The following examples show some of the possible collective bargaining results that may be obtained in the **Settle or Strike** game:

A. Since both teams had agreed on most of the major issues, final agreement on all issues has now been reached. However, the range of concessions made by the company to the union was so heavily weighted in favour of the union that the company has decided to move to another state where it can avoid the union. This will result in direct unemployment of at least 100 men with total annual earnings of over $500,000.

B. Since both teams had agreed on most of the major issues, final agreement on all issues has now been reached. However, the range of concessions made by the union team to the company was so heavily weighted in favour of the company that the union membership refused to ratify the contract and a strike vote was taken which recorded the union in favour of going out on strike. However, bargaining resumed before a strike took effect. Unless the company is willing to concede on the wage and union security issues, prospects for a swift settlement look dim.

C. Since both teams had agreed on most of the major issues, final agreement on all issues was soon reached in subsequent bargaining. However, the range of concessions made by the union team to the company was so heavily weighted in favour of the company that the union membership refused to ratify the contract and decided to strike instead. Moreover, it was the feeling on the part of the union membership that this bargaining team had failed the rank and file and the CWA representation is about to be kicked out unless it can show progress. The strike is continuing at a daily loss of $800 in profits to the company and $1,700 in wages to the employees.

D. Even though the management and union teams have been able to agree on very little in the negotiations so far, they are continuing. Unless there is a change in the stubbornness of both sides to bargain, it is unlikely that any settlement will be reached.

E. Although agreement has been reached, the contract was so heavily weighted in favour of the union that the company simply could not afford to stay in business. Lastik Plastik Company closed down just recently, six months after the agreement was signed. It may reopen in another state sometime in the future. The closing has affected about 100 employees with annual earnings of over $500,000.

F. Since both teams were willing to negotiate in good faith and trade off their less important positions in the interest of agreement, an acceptable settlement has been reached and ratified by the union membership.

●

At the end of the game, when the negotiations have been completed, the instructors and the players should spend some time discussing what was learned by playing SETTLE OR STRIKE. They may come to interesting conclusions that will help them identify some of the important learning needs related to collective bargaining. ■

Carolyn Riding

Reflections on rôle-playing

" *Many people extol the merits of rôle-playing as an aid to workers' education. We are told, for example, how workers can enact the process of joint negotiation, up to the signing of a collective agreement, with some of them filling the rôle of employers and others representing trade union officials. Rightly or wrongly, I do not think a lot of the method ... To ask workers to step out of their own skins, to simulate the reactions of employers, is to demand something completely false of them. They are called upon to think in the manner of an individual who to them is a total outsider. It would be difficult enough for a professional actor for whom the part was written down. For the worker, it invites ridicule, and the lessons supposedly learnt from it can be misleading.*"

Thus wrote one ILO expert in a report on workers' education in Africa.

Strange as it may seem, the more thoughtful advocates of rôle-playing would probably agree with everything he says. Rôle-playing *is* a kind of charade, and therefore false. If students are required to fill rôles they will never occupy in real life, the effect *can* be absurd. And the lessons derived from the game *can* be misleading, if they are not applied with plenty of horse-sense.

The experience of the Kampala Labour College is interesting. At the outset, none of the teachers there were professional educators. They were fairly prominent trade union officials from various countries, combining between them a wealth of practical experience. Several of them had a gift for simple exposition developed in years of trade union debate and discussion. All of them realised that they were learning the art of teaching as they went along. Frequent staff meetings were held to review methods and techniques.

At first, they mounted rôle-playing exercises having all the faults described by the above-quoted expert. The college studies flow in two broad streams. The one covers trade union principles and practice, leading on to collective bargaining procedures; the other embraces basic economics, including elementary statistics, and culminates in the preparation of material in support of trade union objectives. The two streams finally merge in one grand rôle-playing exercise in which the students are required to prepare a statement of claim and argue it across the negotiating table.

For this purpose, they are divided into suitable teams, the transport workers in one team, the public service employees in another team, the plantation workers in a third, the metal workers in a fourth, and so on. Each team is given a dossier of information, including annual company reports, government estimates, details of the existing wage-structure and a copy of the current collective agreement if one exists. They know by now where to go for the background facts—cost of living index, national wage movements, state of the economy, etc. At the end of the exercise, each team is expected to come up with a new collective agreement, sealed and signed.

At first, a group of three students was chosen to simulate the employers' delegation in each case, and the instructor's rôle was to sit in a corner, making notes for a subsequent appraisal. The results were delightful, but not exactly one hundred per cent. pedagogically rewarding. Some of the students taking the employers' side played their parts with tremendous gusto, thumping the table till it squeaked. Others mumbled and were ill at ease, conceding the workers' claims with little argument. Others tried hard to behave as they thought reasonable but tough employers would behave, but they privately considered the phrase " reasonable employer " to be nonsensical and hardly knew, therefore, what it was they were attempting to do. In all cases, the performance was false and any lessons the " workers " thought they learned from their successes or failures with such " employers " were indeed misleading.

The next step was to appoint one of the instructors as the employers' chairman, with two students making up the delegation. This was better, but is was found that the student " employers " took hardly any part in the exercise, leaving it all to the instructor.

When he tried to involve them, by turning to them with some such remark as, " Perhaps one of my colleagues would be good enough to explain our position on this clause ", they were utterly crestfallen and could only gape helplessly from face to face. The " workers " then hooted at them across the table and the session ended in gales of good-natured laughter. This could have been improved, no doubt, with better briefing, but after much argument the instructors decided that was not the answer.

The third step was to use the instructor as sole representative of the employer, with all the students where they really belonged—on the workers' side of the table. On the whole, this worked very well, though it was hard on the instructor, who had to sustain his rôle single-handed.

The final refinement came when representatives of the Uganda Employers Federation were persuaded to play the part of management in some of the industrial negotiations, while Ministry of Labour officials took the executive side in the public service sector. It should be remembered that the Kampala Labour College is an international school, ninety per cent. of the students coming from other countries. The Uganda employers, therefore, were able to join in without actually facing their own people, so to speak. Everybody survived this experience in remarkably high spirits.

The negotiations lasted two or three days, with each side requesting adjournments from time to time to " consult their executives " and draw up revised proposals. Finally, there was a thorough post-mortem, in which the lessons supposedly learned from the exercise were appraised.

A good example of simple rôle-playing practice is given by an ILO expert who used the technique in a short course in West Africa. Two shop-steward situations were enacted as part of a series of practical exercices.

In one exercise, an imaginary incident was created with a worker who was 40 minutes late through over-sleeping. The foreman sacked him on arrival. The brief was that the worker was a militant trade union member, often arguing with the foreman about conditions of work, especially safety. He had already been late once the previous week but the reason was that he had two sick children who were disturbing his sleep. Otherwise, he had not been late in five years with the firm.

In the first scene the worker sees his shop-steward and claims that he is being victimised because of his complaints about safety. In the second, the shop steward is with the manager putting the case for the worker and attempting to obtain his reinstatement. In the third, the shop steward explains to the worker what has been decided. *In every case the student played the rôle of shop steward and the tutor took the opposite rôle.*

In the second exercice the incident concerned a worker who had been caught smoking near a petrol storage tank and who had been sacked on the spot. The brief was that it was against the rules to smoke and that some notices to this effect were posted around the area. The man had worked in the depot for a period of six months without previous fault but he was illiterate. At the same time, the union had been pressing for more safety precautions to protect their members. The worker was complaining of victimisation and applying for reinstatement.

Again, the only part the students were called upon to play was that of the shop steward —the office for which they were being trained. The tutor filled the other rôles. Also in both exercises, the group was small enough *for each member to take his turn as shop steward.* And in both cases there was a thorough discussion afterwards of the points that had emerged. One tutor, for example, was criticised for having consented, in his rôle of manager, to the reinstatement of the cigarette-smoking worker in the second incident, the general view being that the worker merited some punishment—a month's suspension for example—in view of the importance of safety regulations.

" This small incident ", observes the expert, " illustrates one of the beneficial elements in rôle-playing—the fact that personal identification can take place without principles being ignored."

* * *

Some broad guidelines emerge. They cannot always be followed, but they are a useful check :

1. **Students should play the parts they would normally occupy in real life.**
2. **Rôle-playing should not be introduced until students have had sufficient training, or experience, to make the exercise worth while.**
3. **The basic situation should be credible, if not actually true.**

4. **Basic documents should be genuine, if possible. There may be occasions when instructors wish to test the students' acumen in some respect that can best be done by using a carefully prepared document containing, for example, specious arguments, wrongly used statistics, or facts whose true significance is only revealed by careful investigation. Even in such cases there should be no trickery: the students must feel that the document *could have been* real.**

5. **The development of the situation should ring absolutely true. The temptation to over-dramatise, or wilfully introduce comedy, must be resisted. In most episodes there are key rôles which in fact control the evolution of the drama. These should be played by experienced persons who can be relied upon to maintain the authentic note. If necessary, these key actors should be carefully briefed beforehand on the reactions required in given situations. If this is done, the final dénouement will also be " true "—if the students have learned their lessons properly.**

6. **Every student should be involved in a significant way.**

7. **Subsequently, there should be a thorough post-mortem, in which everybody joins. This is one of the most important parts of the exercise. Here, false lessons are discarded, true lessons emphasised, faulty perspectives corrected and points that have been missed can be brought out. Here the good teacher comes into his own again.**

•

There can surely be no argument as to the value of practical exercises, whatever the subject of study. The student-pianist can practise on his own instrument—the real thing—but if the art you are learning involves the human situation, your instruments are men and women, whose reactions are not as predictable as those of the pianoforte. The real thing cannot be provided, yet practise is desirable. Rôle-playing simply makes the best of this irresolvable contradiction.

It is not a new idea. Armies in every country of the world go in for manœuvres, vast rôle-playing exercises in which their officers try to practice the theories they have studied in the lecture theatre. No doubt they would learn better in real battles—but short of actually killing each other what are they to do?

Robert Plant

Some of our workers' educator readers may wish to subscribe their personal views and experiences in the field of rôle-playing. We shall look forward to receiving and publishing any such comments.

Plea on behalf of role-playing

J.V. MORIN
Canadian Union of Public Employees
Former Expert of the International Labour Office

The article by Robert Plant, published in No. 4 of "Labour Education" expressed certain reservations concerning role-playing as a method of labour education. The author recounted certain unfortunate experiences and concluded by listing the snares that had to be avoided if use were made of role-playing.

Initially somewhat annoyed by this article on a method which is close to my heart, and recalling my own experience, I later recognised that basically I was in agreement with the author on more than one point. The essential is to reach agreement on the point of departure of opposite approaches. As far as I am concerned, I believe that role-playing involves a discipline which must be scrupulously observed. Otherwise the best thing is to drop it. What seemed highly significant to me is that several of the conclusions drawn by Robert Plant have an oddly close link with certain strict rules which I consider indispensable for the efficient accomplishment of role-playing and which I shall endeavour to analyse here.

A slice of life

1. In labour education role-playing is re-enacting **a slice of trade union life** as faithfully and as spontaneously as possible, some incident involving a specific grievance, a session of an arbitration board, for example.

2. It is indispensable to have the preparation and the performance of the role-playing done under the **supervision of an animator, monitor, or director of the sketch,** who has a good knowledge both of the technique and of the subject under study, as well as of the background in question, so that the link with reality is never lost from sight.

To provoke discussion

3. In preparing and performing role-playing, the principal object should never be overlooked: as I see it, it is to **provoke fruitful discussion,** concerning the material treated. Secondarily, this technique helps arouse a critical frame of mind, and also the feeling of sharing in responsibilities; to a certain extent, likewise, it develops a talent for public speaking.

Preparation of the role-playing

4. To gain the benefits of the secondary effects produced by role-playing, it is preferable to **recruit the players from among the students themselves.**

In the relatively exceptional case of a team of players with a great deal of background experience, it is possible to improvise the role-playing presentation on the spot in order to answer a question raised in the class during a lecture. The lecturer then takes the part of the monitor or director of the sketch, and three students play the parts, one that of the worker who feels he has a grievance, another that of the shop steward, and the third that of the foreman. And away we go.

As a general rule, however, some prior preparation is called for before the representation. It is nearly always important in this way to have brief rehearsals during which the monitor will cut down any words, gestures, or even scenes which seem superfluous to him.

Except in the special circumstances mentioned in the second paragraph of point 12 below, this will always mean quite summary rehearsals. Thus there is no question of writing out and distributing scripts. However, in order that nothing may be forgotten, the monitor may prepare reference cards of the sort which are shown on page 7. He may even prepare a file of these reference cards into which he can dip when need be, and when he has different classes he is called upon to animate.

5. Each of the interpreters is given a role and must enter into the character of the person he will represent: the worker with a grievance, the shop steward, the foreman, etc. To avoid all confusion, it seems to me imperative to identify each player by means of a placard on which his role is identified.

This identification is all the more important when the "actors" are known to the audience and find that they are assigned roles which are not theirs in real life, or when they are called upon to shift parts when performing several role-playing scenes in the course of one and the same class.

6. In order to distinguish him from the players, the monitor need have no placard. Since he is called upon to intervene in a different way (see points 11, 12, 13 and 14), the monitor must refrain from taking on a role.

Performance of the role-playing

In the light of the foregoing remarks, the following rules should also govern the preparing and the performance of role-playing.

7. The scenes must be few in number and uncomplicated, so that the audience does not get confused.

8. The representation should be performed rapidly; if it is dragged out, the attention of the participants might wander.

9. It is worth recalling that role-playing is neither theatre nor pantomime. Therefore we should refrain from jokes or digressions which might distract the audience from the subject under study.

10. The players should act in the most natural and simple way possible. Nevertheless, in order that they may be fully understood and followed by the audience, they must speak louder than ordinarily, and never turn their backs to the class.

The author of the article goodhumoredly organises role-playing with the help of trade union trainees at the Dakar University Institute of Economic Sciences.

11. Before the role-playing scene, it is recommended that the monitor provide a brief introduction to give the setting.

12. In line with points 7 and 8, an effort to present the full background of a subject should be avoided, for example, all the events which underlay a grievance, running from the incident which provoked it to the final settlement. It is sufficient if, by means of brief scenes, the essentials are given. To link these scenes together, the monitor will step in to explain what may have taken place in the meantime – see examples in page 7.

If, under exceptionally favourable circumstances and with a fully trained troupe, a departure from this rule is intended, and it is sought to give a full representation of a collective bargaining session or an arbitration board hearing, it will then be necessary to prepare in advance a script with a copy for each player; the spontaneity may well be diminished. In such cases, it would be desirable to have the monitor cut the scene from time to time so as to call attention to the development of the situation or to the behaviour of a given character.

13. At the end of the representation, the monitor will always call upon the audience to draw conclusions. For example, what would they do in such and such a case?

14. Lastly, the role-playing should make use of a minimum of accessories. In addition to the placards mentioned above, all that will be needed are a table, a few chairs, and at the most a few simple props such as a plastic telephone, when necessary. It is up to the monitor to compensate for the lack of accessories and the absence of scenery.

Advantages of role-playing

- Obviously, role-playing is the least costly of all the audio-visual means.
- As we saw above, it helps to arouse the critical spirit and the feeling of responsibility; it develops oratorical capacities.
- Role-playing is within everybody's reach. Its preparation is simple and brief and requires only the most rudimentary props.
- The pattern is flexible and can be adapted to many a subject of study. Role-playing can provide the practical illustration of certain aspects of the subject dealt with by the lecturer. It can also encourage the participants themselves to discover solutions to the problems raised. It may even be possible, on occasion, intentionally to introduce a few errors in the behaviour

of a trade union leader in order to ascertain whether the audience has fully understood the course and whether it can detect these errors. The monitor will then draw the logical conclusions – see example No. 2 on page 7.

- Even if, as a rule, role-playing should not be turned into a comedy, generally everybody who participates does so with real pleasure. Isn't it desirable, from time to time, to break up the monotony of classes, of study days or of long courses, and to brighten the atmosphere?

A few live experiences

I have, for a long time, been making use of role-playing in workers' circles, both in Canada and in the course of missions entrusted to me by the I.L.O. The results of these experiments obviously varied greatly depending on the milieu.

With my friends in Senegal, who are as voluble as Latins, I had some difficulty in following points 7 and 8. Not that there was any lack of enthusiasm, but often it was necessary to dam the flood of words so that the essential would emerge, and sometimes the representation dragged on too slowly. Thus, paradoxically, eloquence and a ready tongue may be somewhat harmful in role-playing. But, all in all, it has always seemed to me that this method was highly successful in the African situation.

In Ceylon the tea-pickers and the workers in tea mastered this technique very quickly, adapting it to the needs of their workers' education programme, in particular for the formation of the trade union leadership assigned to handle the settlement of grievances.

In the Canadian setting, where my daily work takes place, a certain timidity may, in the beginning, impede role-playing. That is because television has popularised the dramatic art and on that account there is perhaps a certain embarrassment on the part of the workers who have no artistic training to throw themselves into acting a "role". But very quickly the ice is broken and they all join easily in playing the game. In this way role-playing has come into current use in Canada.

Role-playing is nearly always as pleasing to the interpreters as it is to the audience. Nevertheless, we should take care not to consider it as a simple parlour game. If it tends to make people laugh, it is less because of the fact that certain characters are susceptible of being caricatured than it is because of the situations it illustrates which are only too familiar to the spectators: they often find in it a reflection of their everyday life.

TWO EXAMPLES OF MONITOR'S REFERENCE CARD

1. Role-playing dramatising a case of unpaid overtime

3 scenes
4 characters

Scene one

E. D. encounters a fellow worker. She shows him the slip accompanying her bi-weekly pay and is surprised to find that four overtime hours are lacking, two hours for each of the two last Thursday evenings.

Her friend suggests that she speaks about it to her shop steward.

Between the two scenes the monitor explains that Miss D. has followed the advice, that she has explained her grievance to the shop steward and that the following scene will take place in the office of the new foreman.

Scene two

The aggrieved worker and her shop steward come into the office of the foreman. The shop steward points out to the latter that a mistake has been made in the pay of his fellowworker.

The foreman says that, in the two weeks since he has taken over the management of the department, he never asked Miss D. to work after the regular hours. The young woman explains that for the past three years, every Thursday evening, after the other employees have left, she is paid to pick up the dusters and wash them. The foreman answers that there is no reason why he has to ratify the orders that his predecessors may have given and that, as for him, he will only pay overtime when he has given the order to work overtime.

The monitor explains that after this interview, in connection with his investigation and for establishing proof, the shop steward asked Miss D. for additional information.

Scene three

Miss D. comes up to her shop steward in the corridor and turns over to him her salary vouchers for the past three years, which she has kept at home. The shop steward verifies a few of them on the spot and finds that these vouchers do indeed show overtime work on Thursday evenings.

The monitor asks the participants "What would you do in such a case?"

2. Role-playing dramatising a rumour of dismissal

1 or 2 scenes
shop steward and several un-named persons

The monitor explains that the scene takes place in the cloak room while the workers are putting on their work clothes.

Scene one

The shop steward, who is taking off his jacket, is literally taken by assault by his work companions who are cursing and asking him what he is waiting for to defend them and demand respect for their rights.

Disconcerted, the shop steward asks what is happening. "What, don't you know", they retort, "that old G. has just been fired and that this new young puppy of a foreman has been boasting all over the place that he would get rid of all the old employees?"

The monitor asks the class: "What would you do in this case?"

The monitor may then show a second scene, explaining that the shop steward has gone to the superintendent to complain about this firing which he considers unjustified. The second scene therefore takes place in the office of the superintendent.

Scene two — 2 characters

The shop steward outlines his grievance. The superintendent, astonished, replies that he has had no word of any such firing, but that he will check on it. He telephones the foreman and asks him what it is all about. After having hung up, he announces to the shop steward that the employee in question was not fired, but that the truth of the matter is that he obtained leave of absence for personal reasons.

The monitor reminds the class that the expression of a grievance should be based on facts, after enquiry, if need be. He concludes that the shop steward would have done well to inform himself from the outset by questioning the chief person concerned or one of his close friends.

The Organisation of Training Courses for Trade Union Instructors

The Workers' Education Programme of the International Labour Office was conceived as a "diversified and balanced programme of workers' education activities designed to benefit, either directly or indirectly, immediately or in the long run, workers and their organisations". This was the definition given by consultants on workers education in the meeting which was held in Geneva from 7 to 18 December 1964. They also stressed that the I.L.O. should continue to develop activities such as that of training of administrators and instructors, preparation of manuals and study materials, elaboration and supply of audio-visual aids and equipment, granting fellowships and exchange of workers' education personnel, studies undergone by trade unionists relating to educational problems confronting them and, naturally, teaching about the Organisation itself, which the Office is obviously best equipped to provide.

The consultants had emphasised that one of the basic objectives of the I.L.O.'s Workers' Education Programme was "to help trade unions and workers' education bodies to help themselves" in developing their training activities. In this way, the support that is requested by the trade union organisations (or by the institutions set up in collaboration with them), tends to vitalise some action that is responsive to their own needs, and that they must organise and supervise on their own responsibility.

Within this pattern and in the light of these principles, the action of the I.L.O. in helping trade union organisations to set up and develop their own workers' education services amounts to one of the basic forms of assistance provided by the Workers' Education Branch in the various regions of the world and most particularly in Africa. It is a fact that on the African continent the central trade union bodies have not, in general, been able to establish a permanent, autonomous and systematic education service which is adequate to meet the demands of the educational tasks and needs of the trade union movement; this is due to the meagreness of their material equipment, the limited number of their trained staff, and to the overwhelming complexity of various other demands and responsibilities confronting them.

A pattern for intervention

Little by little the African trade union organisations – aided by the I.L.O. – are becoming aware that they must now replace the sporadic and somewhat unorganised educational activities which they have been carrying on either by themselves or with such assistance as they were able to get from outside, and set up a training system which would keep in pace with the progress achieved by the students and would be adapted to the various levels involving responsibility. One of the chief difficulties which they must overcome, is the **absence or virtually complete lack of qualified educators.** The help given by the I.L.O. to these organisations has therefore gradually become channelled so as to give priority to the training of trade union instructors in labour education. This is accomplished by regional experts where each assists a certain number of trade union organisations in the region to which they are assigned.

In the light of the instruction given to them through the Seminar on the Development of Workers' Education in the ex-French Territories of Western and Central Africa and Madagascar (held in Douala, November-December 1963), and later through the Experimental Project to Assist the Development of Workers' Education (held in July 1964 to June 1965), the pattern for the intervention of the I.L.O. experts in a given country was broadly outlined as follows:

- **First phase:** one or more visits made by experts to the authorities and the trade union organisations of the country, for the purpose of studying with them the ways and means of setting up a workers' education service and preparing an educational programme;
- **Second phase:** the organisation and direction of a training period for animators and instructors in workers' education, so as to give the participants the necessary technical preparation for applying the selected educational programme;
- **Third phase:** one or more visits by the expert for the purpose of advising the animators and instructors while they are carrying out their programmes;
- **Fourth phase:** the organisation and direction of an advanced period and a refresher course for the group of instructors trained during the period composing the second phase of the operation.

Thus the training course for instructors in workers' education is at the hub of the drive undertaken by the I.L.O. to assist the trade union organisations in equipping themselves with an educational service. The first aim of the expert's intervention is to ensure the psychological and technical preparation of the course, and the two last aims provide the support and inspiration of the instructors as well as their professional improvement.

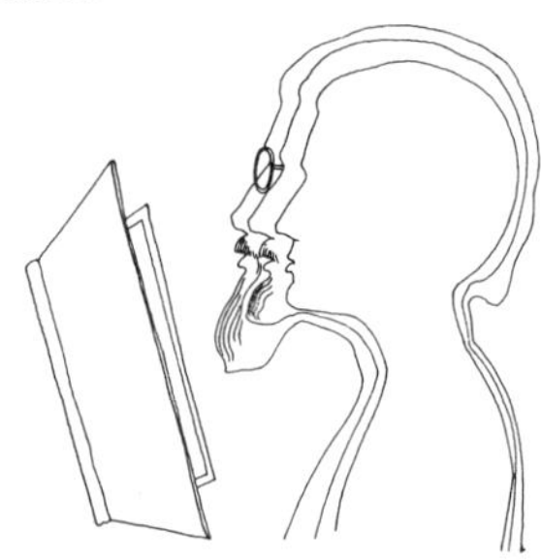

A continual improvement

The Training Programme

In the above outlined pattern, the preparation of trade union instructors for workers' education is not limited to the teaching given to them during the training course alone. In fact, the latter is immediately followed by a programme of educational work assigned to the candidate instructor, which he is committed to fulfil. This programme is intended to provide him with the possibility of making **concrete application** of the teaching he has received, a bit of **personal experience** in the educational process and especially **self-confidence,** which is a decisive element for the continuance of the activities undertaken. Naturally the expert must supervise the work, check it, animate it, correct the errors, help to eliminate the obstacles which are too difficult for the beginner instructor to handle himself, and, guide him towards a career of a worker educator.

It goes without saying that the training of the instructor must be followed, after this practical experience, by a subsequent period of perfecting his skills and refreshing his knowledge on the teaching given in the training course itself and equipping him with the basis for a programme of longer duration and greater variety of applications. These two stages are integral to the process of training trade union instructors, quite as much as the course itself. They mark a culminating point, and the I.L.O. is aware that the educators prepared in this way will have to integrate themselves in an endless process of individual training and a continual improvement. Further means will then have to be employed: pedagogical instruction on the use of audio-visual aids, on specialisation, study trips abroad, etc.; the I.L.O. will endeavour to arrange for fitting assistance in so far as its means permit.

The programme of the instructor training course is prepared in collaboration with the I.L.O. expert and the trade union organisation which has called for his services, or, when there are several trade union centres in a country which wish to profit from that course, by the I.L.O. expert and an inter-trade union organisation committee set up for the purpose. While always making an adaptation to the local circumstances, the programme is generally based on the following elements:

- a student body of some 20 to 25 participants;
- a duration of about four weeks;
- an intensive full-time schedule, with a student boardinghouse wherever possible.

The fixed quota is prescribed according to the optimum conditions for teaching, which are based on methods of active participation and needs and possibilities of a trade union central body of average size. As for the duration, while it seems impossible to cut down the time, because of the minimum programme to be given, it appears, that this is the maximum which can be taken on an intensive basis by participants who are not accustomed to this sort of intellectual effort. The full-time schedule is ideal for candidates from various parts of the country, who come to make the best use of their time.

Three distinct parts or aspects normally make up the programme of a training course for trade union instructors:

- study of the organisation and operation of a trade union service for workers' education;
- practical teaching of the methods and techniques used in workers' education;
- basic training on the subjects which the future workers' education instructors will be teaching.

A variety of experiences have proved that it is absolutely necessary to continue giving instruction on the first phase, devoted to the organisation of workers' education services if we wish to see the training course results in a commitment on the part of the participants and if we wish the trade unions to follow up the course with concrete action and initiative. This phase, preceded by an introductory lesson on the "necessity of workers' education", is customarily given in four reports extensively discussed in the working groups, their subjects being:

- workers' education on various levels;
- the responsible organs for workers' education in a trade union central body;
- the establishment of a workers' education centre;
- how to find the resources needed for workers' education.

Reports are prepared, based on group discussion, which are later taken up in the plenary session.

The second part of the course, devoted to the teaching of workers' education methods and techniques, is without any doubt the most important, since, in the last analysis, the purpose of the course is to teach trade union militants **how to communicate their knowledge to their fellow workers.** In other words, it is a question of getting the future instructors to prepare and to present a report, to direct a meeting-discussion, to make proper use of audio-visual aids and pedagogical methods adapted to teaching adult workers.

It appeared preferable to drop any theoretical lessons on methods and techniques of workers' education and even their demonstrations, but this has not yet been fully accomplished, because of the lack of fully prepared experts. Whereas one demonstration may be sufficient for the leaders who have no special need to know what it is all about, when it comes to the instructors, they must be able to handle practically these methods and techniques, or at least the commonest and most effective ones. The expert will provide a far better insight into them if he utilises the various methods and techniques in presenting the different subjects on the programme, and in this way he will get the participants to recognise the merits and effectiveness of each of them.

It is also necessary to have a guide in the field of technical materials in order to avoid dependence on complicated devices which are beyond the means of small and poor trade union organisations, or which cannot be adapted for use under local conditions. For this reason the episcope and even the 16 mm projector must give way, in most cases, to the film strip, tape recorder and blackboard. In some places the flannelboard is practical, or the flip chart, if the necessary elements can be found to illustrate the lessons which are being studied. The methods used must also be simple: a thorough understanding of the lecture, presented with a blackboard for notes, a trained group leader, the use of team investiga-

Training at Douala (April 1968). A lecture on the blackboard dealing with methods of work (M. Etoundi)

tion and a few modest audio-visual aids are entirely adequate to begin with.

Naturally, after these methods and materials have been used by an experienced leader of the course, the future instructors should have a chance for practical work in order to train themselves in the use of these elements. This aspect of the training programme for instructors is essential and the experience of the I.L.O. leads it to devote more and more time to it. This practical work is a most important part of the training because it gives them confidence in their capacity as educators. But how can this be brought about, considering all the other materials which are necessary to be included in the programme? Without pretending to have a ready solution, the Workers' Education Branch gives its experts the following advice:

- eliminate all theoretical lessons on the methods and technical aspects of workers' education;
- reduce the number of lectures and conferences dealing with elementary trade union education;
- assign more preparatory work for the practical sessions to be done by the students outside class hours;
- perform certain practical exercises, not on an individual basis, but in small groups of three or four persons;
- limit the length of time of each of the practical exercises (speaking from the floor, presentation of a speech) in order to increase their number.

The third part of the training course for trade union instructors provides basic training on trade unionism. The question has often been asked as to whether this training is indispensable, and if it is, what subject should be studied, and how much importance should be given to it. Experience has provided the answer to the first part of the question, because the general level of education of the participants demands that they receive elementary training in the subjects which they will teach in the future, since the trainees are not experienced leaders, but militants drawn from the rank and file. In addition, even when they are very familiar with the subject matter, it is helpful to organise and clarify their thinking and to provide them with an outline which will act as a memorandum to help them in the proper presentation of the subject matter when they teach their own students later on. And finally, it is very difficult to try to teach abstract pedagogical method without applying it to a particular subject.

A common fund

The answer to the question of what should be taught in a course on trade unionism is much more complicated and delicate, and in the past certain trade unions have even challenged the right of the I.L.O. to deal with this type of education. The I.L.O. consultants on workers' education, meeting in Geneva in December 1964, said that education in this field could be considered as the **common fund** for all the information necessary to all the unions, no matter what their philosophic and political orientation might be. Therefore, it must include, in its programme, certain specific studies concerning:

- **the trade union** – its structure, its organisation, its role; why join a trade union; the rights and the responsibilities of the trade unionists;
- **the enterprise** – its aims, its organisation, its role; the place of the worker and workers' representative in the enterprise;
- **labour law** and collective bargaining agreements;
- **social security;**
- **workers' health and safety, etc.**

The teaching level should be sufficiently high to permit the trade union trainee instructor to feel completely competent to give an **introductory course on trade unionism,** without going beyond this. At least at the beginning, it is superfluous to try to stuff the instructors with information or involve them in complexities; they may find it impossible to distinguish the really important elements. It is only by means of refresher courses, which form the fourth phase of the programme for training instructors, that it will be possible to advance the teaching of the trainees to a higher level. Moreover, experience shows that active instructors become rapidly aware of their inadequacies and they call for more advanced training themselves, particularly on economic questions.

Training Techniques and Methods

The teaching methods used in the instructors training course should be an application of the methods and techniques of worker's education which are to be taught to the future instructors. In other words, what is to be taught is both the **subject** and **the way of communicating it** to the future students. In order not to separate the one from the other, it is worth while to frequently alter the methods and techniques of teaching so that the participants become familiar with those most commonly used. As an example of this, the I.L.O. experts made use of the following pedagogical means in a recent instructors training course held in Niamey[1].

- **course using the blackboard:** cycle on the organisation of workers' education, for example;
- **lecture followed by discussion:** dealing with trade union organisation;
- **debate:** with the directors of the Women's Union of the Niger on the role of women in the social structure;
- **group or committee work:** thorough analysis of all the speeches; preparation of an educational programme of introduction to trade unionism;
- **course with flannelboard:** the enterprise (structure and operation), organisation of the trade union;
- **film strip:** the role of the shop steward using the film strip made by the Malay unions, "How Trade Unions Settle their Grievances";
- **role-playing** (or stage acting): legislation on the representation of personnel in the enterprises;
- **visit:** social security (starting with a visit to the Niamey Office of Social Security);
- **team investigation:** research and use of data; socio-economic analysis of an enterprise (based on two visits to factories in Niamey).

Notes must be usable

In addition to the fact that the teaching given in this varied form is far more interesting to the participants, it gives them some idea of the diverse methods available to workers' education and a basis of comparison of their effectiveness. Naturally, it is desirable to round off this presentation with practical work which should include, in our view, the following exercises:

- **taking notes;**
- **drafting and presenting a report (group report, visit, investigation, etc.);**
- **handling and guiding group projects;**
- **preparation of speeches;**
- **how to give a speech in public;**
- **how to present a subject, using the blackboard;**
- **how to use a projector and how to present film strips or slides;**
- **how to use the tape recorder.**

Among all the various methods and techniques used in instructors training courses, the one which seems most effective is **group or committee work,** supplementing a lesson given in any of the above-mentioned manners. This truly allows the lesson to be seen in a different manner. It becomes possible to give it thorough individual analysis, to test it against a series of personal experiences, to synthesise different points of view, without even mentioning the practical activity involved: leadership and animation of the discussion, summarisation of a debate, editing, and presenting

[1] *See* Labour Education, *No. 13, June 1968.*

conclusions and preparing a report, public speaking. The individual progress achieved by the trainees is quite spectacular, sometimes exceeding even the most optimistic expectations. But it is clear that these results depend on the technique at the command of the group leaders. Therefore, the leadership should not be entrusted to inexperienced participants except for their practical and supervised training, otherwise the results will be uninteresting and useless.

The **flannelboard** technique has been used by the I.L.O. experts and has proved highly effective for certain course subjects in which a visual presentation can be given, for instance, an economic cycle. A course on "The Enterprise – what it is; how it operates" handled in this way at Niamey was considered to be most attractive and most comprehensible by the majority of the participants. But this method requires considerable preliminary preparation (at least the first time), rehearsals, and a good command of public speaking. The same is true of the use of the flip chart, which resembles flannelboard technique in many ways. It seems almost useless to teach this method unless we can supply the future instructors with the designed material, together with instructions for use and a more or less rigid text which the designs illustrate.

To keep contact with trainees use flannelboard

Next, **team investigation** seems to be a particularly interesting method because of its various practical applications, which teach people how to see and evaluate facts. We felt that the teams should make more use of factory visits or social institutions, which are frequent features of the instructors courses. Such visits are not always very important in themselves, and easily degenerate into mere entertainment. If, however, a small group of trainees is called upon to make an investigation before the visit, this totally modifies their attitude toward what they see, and directs their curiosity to the human and social facts. The subsequent work carried out jointly: comparing the notes taken, interpreting the data, editing the reports, is likewise most fruitful.

We should also stress how greatly the use of **role-playing,** or acting out a common trade union activity, gives excellent results, especially in Africa where we find born actors with the true flame. The participants enter into the spirit of the scene very rapidly, blending fiction and reality with great skill. Here too, much depends on the animator: he can't always avoid "hamming", nor wasting a lot of time in palaver that drifts far from the subject. But since, in the long run, this is handled according to the methods and thinking habits consistent with the customs and the native genius of those involved, we finally succeed in having a concrete adaptation of what the experts are teaching. This, furthermore, makes it possible to judge how fully the participants have assimilated the instruction.

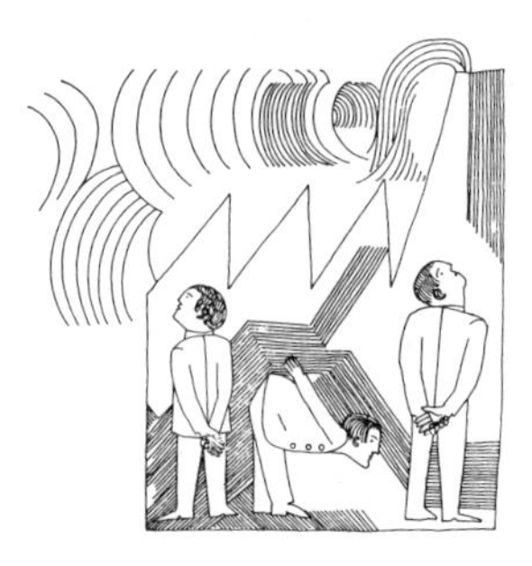

Team investigation: a slice of life

The **film strip** (or series of slides) can be a pedagogical aid of primary interest, both in training instructors and in training their future pupils, if we have strips or series adaptable to the subject taught. In various recent courses in Africa, a speech on the role of shop stewards was successfully given, using a film strip made by the Malay trade unions entitled "How Trade Unions Settle their Grievances". The drawings are humorous, but not overly so; the factory scenes which it presents, even the clothing of the personnages, are not too individualised, and since there is no written text, it is possible to fit in a commentary consistent with the laws and the actual situation in the new country where the material is being used. This adaptation of a text to accord with both the pictures and the subject of the course is a fairly difficult task which usually cannot be entrusted to the trainees.

Evaluation of the Results

It is difficult to make exact evaluation of the results achieved in the training of instructors for workers' education from the above-outlined method, for the various phases of such training have only been completed for a limited number of instructors, and the preparation of worker educators is a continuous process, and an endless task.

However, the instructor training course outlined above and the pedagogical methods it brings into play make it impossible to measure the individual progress of the participants in the training periods, **provided that the candidates' initial knowledge has attained a certain level** below which it would be impossible for them to fully benefit from the courses given.

Here we tackle a problem familiar to all those who are responsible for trade union education services: that of the homogeneity of the group taught. This means the prior selection of the instructor-candidates. In recent courses of this nature, the expert found his work difficult and the results devaluated by the considerable differences in level among the participants, whose education went all the way from primary school to a college degree, and preliminary training for teaching work – all the way from nothing to pedagogical consultant for primary schools, including candidates who had followed one or more training courses abroad. To cope with the difficulty of ensuring a form of instruction equally profitable to all, under such conditions, it was decided to improve the selection of teaching instructors, as far as possible, and for this purpose it was decided:

- to state the requirements of such a selection more frankly to the responsible trade union movement, when the programme is being prepared;
- to include the I.L.O. expert, as Director of the course, in the selection committee assigned to choose the candidates for training as instructors;
- to have all the candidates complete an information sheet prior to the selection. This would help to make a more cohesive choice of the participants.

The Workers' Education Branch understands that a better selection of future instructors calls for a genuine and far-reaching collaboration of trade union movement leaders who wish to set up or to develop education activities. They must be willing to make the necessary effort and sacrifice, especially in terms of human resources, all of which presupposes a growth in understanding on the part of both the trade union leaders and the militants, on the part of the public authorities and public opinion in general. As a result, it seems necessary to give greater importance in the future to this first phase of the expert's intervention, and to ask him to prepare the psychological ground thoroughly so as to obtain a full commitment, not only from the national trade union leaders, but also from the

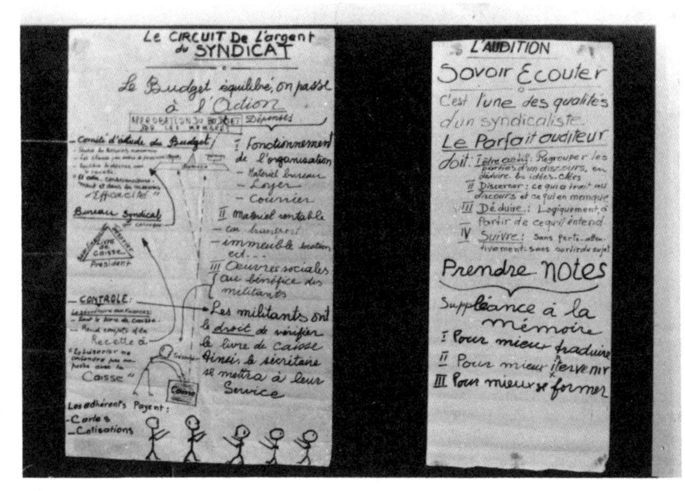

Flipcharts prepared by two trainees at Douala (Messrs. Ngoubeme and Mgassam)

authorities concerned, and even, to a certain extent, from the employers. More frequent contacts with the various groups, study days, conferences and work sessions on labour education at the various levels of the trade union movement, an informational drive among the authorities and public opinion are among the means contemplated to achieve this goal.

Don't put the film in the wrong way

Problems to be solved

In addition, improvements can still be made in the present system of the trade union instructors' training course, especially as regards the programme, teaching of workers' education methods and techniques, the material to be taught, the documentation to be given to the participants. But one point which is of special interest to the I.L.O. Workers' Education Branch is the difficulty of finding experts who are capable of mastering the various worker-training techniques they themselves must teach to the candidates. Such preparation in the modern methods of educating workers is quite rare. As a result, plans are being made to work out a pedagogical training course which enables trainees to get this education, and instructors to further advance in this difficult field.

As for the actual material to be taught, the problem which has preoccupied the I.L.O. is that of the **course outlines,** which appear to be absolutely necessary material for the new instructors in helping them to develop their presentations of labour education subjects. Should they be given relatively complete and extensive texts, or only the course outline of what the instructor should do, limited to the level of an introduction to trade unionism, as we have said before? In the past, the outlines given to the participants have tried to be both a memorandum on the teaching which had been given to them and a guide for the courses which they will have to present in turn. Perhaps it would be desirable to separate these two functions. The ideal might be to present first a clear and well-organised summary of the basic ideas which have been studied, and next, a detailed plan for the suggested course to be taught.

Lastly, despite everything which has been done so far, we cannot be unaware of the scarcity of audio-visual material adapted to the requirements for training instructors, as well as those for the training of their future students. The problem which the I.L.O. must solve is how to prepare elements which can be used in all circumstances, keeping in mind the very wide variety in the ways of looking at things, and the differences in esthetic requirements. The national organisations work out their own projects in terms of their own needs and the circumstances prevailing in their own countries – which is natural. We mentioned above the good results obtained with a Malayan film strip which was designed in such a way that commentaries could be easily adapted to the pictures. This is true of a few others from Indian sources on trade unions and the formation of co-operatives. Certain film strips illustrating trade union techniques, prepared in Europe, are also usable. They deal with the operation of the duplicator, with the organisation and direction of a trade union meeting, with the role of the shop steward or the trade union, etc. But how is it possible, in the heart of Africa, to adapt an excellent film strip on collective bargaining, prepared for the use of Canadian trade unions? As for 16 mm moving pictures, the choice is even more limited. And those which can provide a basis for teaching given to workers in the developing countries are rare.

I.L.O. experts and outside specialists find, on the basis of their experience, that it would be extremely useful to be able to have film strips, series of slides, sets of drawings to be used with the flannelboard and lesson outlines, produced as rapidly as possible, and to send them to the trade unions and central bodies concerned with workers' education. These valuable pedagogical instruments, too often dumped into the bottom of closets, would then become accessible to all the worker-educators who wish to serve their fellow workers.

By giving priority to "training the trainers" as the I.L.O. consultants wanted, the Workers' Education Branch has a difficult task. But when, just about everywhere, we see teams emerging which devote themselves to the training of the workers and which keep on organising educational activities in all the countries in which this preparation of instructors has taken place, we have the right to think that this toilsome pathway may well, in the final analysis, be the only one that can lead to the rise of an enlightened and responsible labour movement.

Robert Vautherin

Sample Programme for a Seminar on Training of Trade Union Instructors

FIRST WEEK

Day	Session	Activity
Monday:		Inauguration.
Tuesday:	morning –	Presentation of the course – explanations about its projected pattern and its method of work.
		The I.L.O. and its activities – projection of the filmstrip on the I.L.O. – discussion.
	evening –	Need for workers' education – group work – reports of the groups.
Wednesday:	morning –	Trade union training at the various levels – lecture and discussion – group work.
	evening –	Reports by the groups.
		Practical work: setting up a programme of introduction to trade unionism.
Thursday:	morning –	The responsible bodies for workers' education – lecture and discussion – group work.
	evening –	Reports by the groups. Practical work: how to take notes.
Friday:	morning –	Establishment of educational centres by the trade union central bodies. How to find the means to finance needs of workers' education – lecture and discussion – group work.
	evening –	Reports by the groups. Practical work: preparing and presenting a speech.
Saturday:	morning –	The enterprise – lecture – discussion.

SECOND WEEK

Day	Session	Activity
Monday:	morning –	The trade union – lecture – discussion.
		Group work.
	evening –	The trade union – reports by the groups.
		Practical work: presentation of course by trainees.
Tuesday:	morning –	Visit to a Social Security Office.
	evening –	Social security – lecture – questions and discussion.
Wednesday:	morning –	The shop steward – presentation of the filmstrip: "How Trade Unions settle their Grievances" – lecture and discussion.
	evening –	Session of role-playing: election of the shop stewards (trade union preparation – demands – elections).
Thursday:	morning –	Practical work: presentation of course by trainees.
	evening –	Trade union organisation – lecture – discussion.
		The enterprise (demonstration of the flannelboard).
Friday:	morning –	Practical work: presentation of speeches.
	evening –	Visit to two enterprises (team investigations).
Saturday:	morning –	Trade union finances – lecture – discussion.

THIRD WEEK

Day	Session	Activity
Monday:	morning –	The Labour Code and the social laws of the country – lecture – group work – discussion – reports by the groups.
	evening –	Practical work: presentation of course by trainees.
Tuesday:	morning –	Reports of investigations during visits to enterprises.
	evening –	Practical work: presentation of speeches by trainees.
Wednesday:	morning –	Labour inspection – lecture – group work and discussion.
	evening –	Practical work.
Thursday:	morning –	Role of women in society (debate).
	evening –	Practical work: presentation of speeches by trainees.
Friday:	morning –	The plan for development of the country – discussion.
	evening –	Practical work: presentation of speeches by trainees.

FOURTH WEEK

Day	Session	Activity
Monday:	morning –	The audio-visual Centre and its participation in workers' education.
		The association of radio clubs in the country. Speeches followed by debate.
	evening –	Rural animation – lecture followed by questions and discussion.
Tuesday:	morning –	Organisation of future educative activities: presentation by the participants of plans for work.
	evening –	Evaluation of the seminar.
Wednesday:	morning –	Closing session.

Federal Republic of Germany

Integrated Teaching Methods in Trade Union Training on Wage and Work Study Problems

While trade union activities cover an ever-increasing field, wages and working conditions are still within the focus of collective bargaining and day-to-day union activities. Wage determination has become a rather complex subject which involves the application of fairly sophisticated methods derived from work study and industrial engineering techniques. This is true even of developing countries where western industrial enterprises try to implant schemes of piece rates based on time study, bonus schemes, job evaluation, and systems of measured-day work, just to mention a few.

Hans PORNSCHLEGEL
Head of the DGB Federal School,
Bad Kreuznach

There is also another difficulty: the bargaining partners on the employers' side are becoming more and more sophisticated. This makes bargaining and the implementation of agreed systems more and more difficult. On the other hand, workers' representatives get more and more involved in the problems of the daily running of such schemes. Grievances arise, alterations have to be made and new solutions have to be found. This cannot be done without thorough training meeting the standards necessary to maintain the status and security of the workers represented in the enterprise.

Since training in these fields is not just a matter of technicalities and formulas, it has to be practical and up to date. Trade union training in these fields has to utilise all feasible teaching methods within the reach of the organisations, depending on the stage of development of industry and unions. Within the Deutscher Gewerkschaftsbund (German Trade Union Federation, Federal Republic of Germany), training in these fields is carried out by the autonomous affiliated trade unions as well as by the DGB Federal School, Bad Kreuznach, in pilot courses, advanced courses and specialised seminars which form part of the general programme offered to active members.

This article tries to indicate some of the recent trends in thinking and experimentation.

Role of educational planning

The DGB is trying to overhaul its educational system in order to render efficient and valuable services to the membership of its affiliated unions. As part of these efforts new plans have been made for the training of officers in the field of collective bargaining, wage and salary determination and work study. The aims and content of this training should be based on functions exercises. Trade union training is considered as the system determined to implement these aims and contents which are identical with the functions and offices held within the trade union organisations. The elements of this system, i.e. teachers, students and teaching aids, should be put to optimal use by applying the most adequate and efficient methods.

But how to determine the aims and contents of such training? The planning system has recourse to vocational training, where detailed functional descriptions are used for the determination of curricula. The functions described, based on practical inquiries, include:

1. A general description of the functions to be exercised;
2. A definition of the starting level of general and specialised information and experiences;
3. The individual tasks to be fulfilled within the function. These tasks are defined at a minimal and at an optimal level:
   (a) the minimal level characterises the minimal requirements necessary to fulfil the function;
   (b) the optimal level indicates the long-range tasks as defined by the trade union strategy;
4. The information required to exercise these tasks;
5. The necessary mental, technical, manual and social skills (figure A).

The plan was inspired by Nadler's system approach in certain industrial engineering fields. Instead of improving existing systems here and there, Nadler suggests a fresh approach and the planning of an ideal system, in this case for training purposes. Such an ideal system, based on the tasks to be performed, would guarantee ideally the transfer of information and skills. Since this ideal is impossible to achieve, the system has to be shaped in the form of a model, which has to be related to the currently existing situation in the field of training (figure B).

The DGB Federal School at Bad Kreuznach is co-ordinating efforts to publish a handbook for workers' representatives dealing with wages and working conditions at plant and regional levels. The handbook will form the nucleus of existing and new teaching materials and aids. Information theory, some cybernetic starting points and sociological aspects will be included in a digestible form.

Co-ordination of teaching aids and teaching methods

So that the teaching process will be as effective as possible, some conditions have to be fulfilled to achieve the objectives set:

1. The over-all and partial objectives of teaching have to be clearly and explicitly defined;
2. Priorities among the different objectives have to be decided upon;
3. The alternatives of different combinations of teaching aids and methods have to be tested and adequate ones have to be selected.

Among the many combinations of teaching aids and methods applied on an experimental basis, some will be described below.

During the past ten years the DGB Federal School has produced about ninety 16 mm films. They are mostly documentary films of operations and work situations. They have been widely used for cases in time and motion study as well as job evaluation. For most of the subjects in the field of wage determination and work study, filmstrips with sound tracks have been prepared. These materials have been and are still quite popular among the trade unions within their own training courses and seminars.

During the past few years some integrated methods were given a predominant role and pro-

The DGB Federal School at Bad Kreuznach

FIGURE A. – THE ANALYSIS OF FUNCTIONAL SCOPES AND THEIR BEARING ON TEACHING OBJECTIVES AND PROCESSES

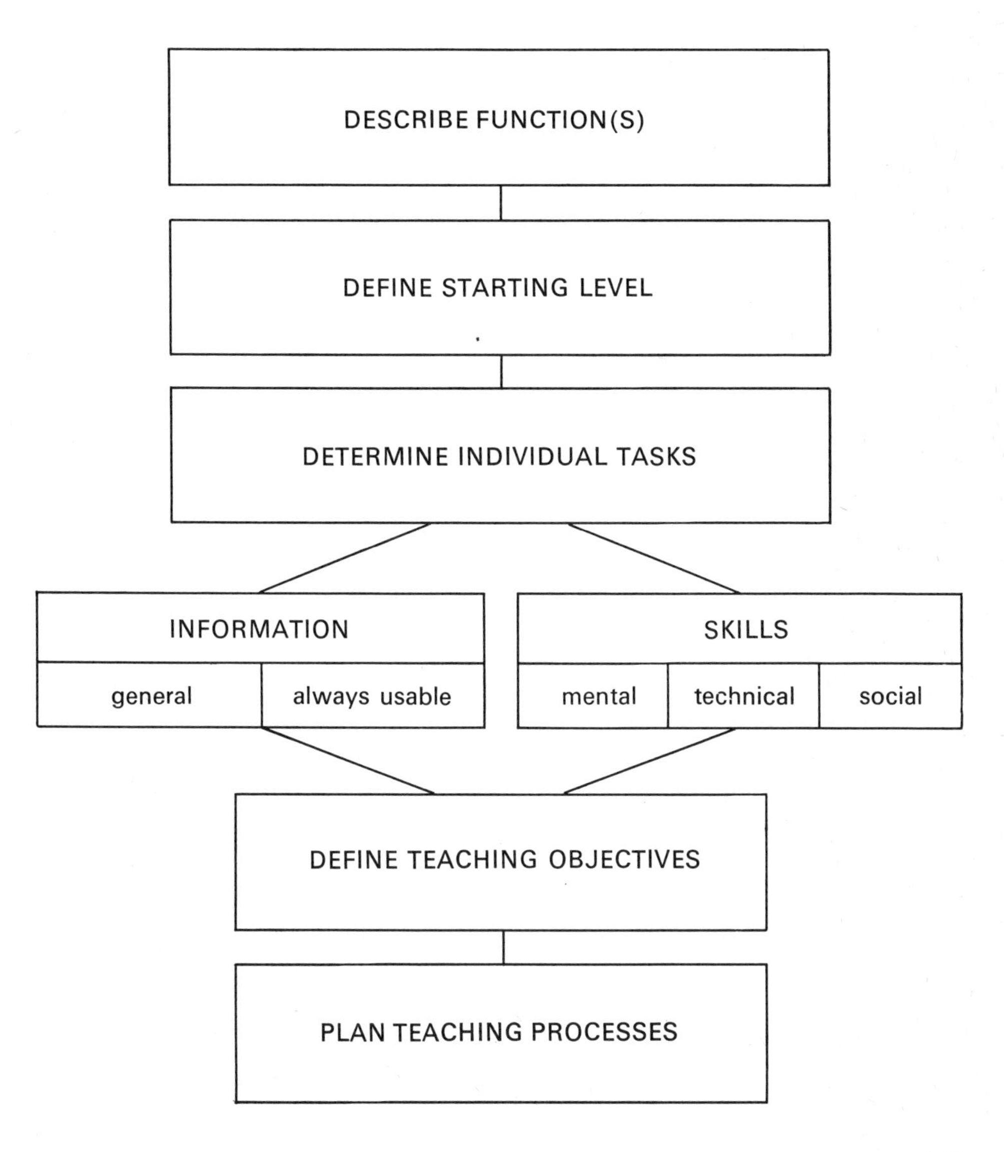

FIGURE B. – COMPARISON OF CONVENTIONAL AND SYSTEMS APPROACH IN IMPROVING EDUCATIONAL SYSTEMS

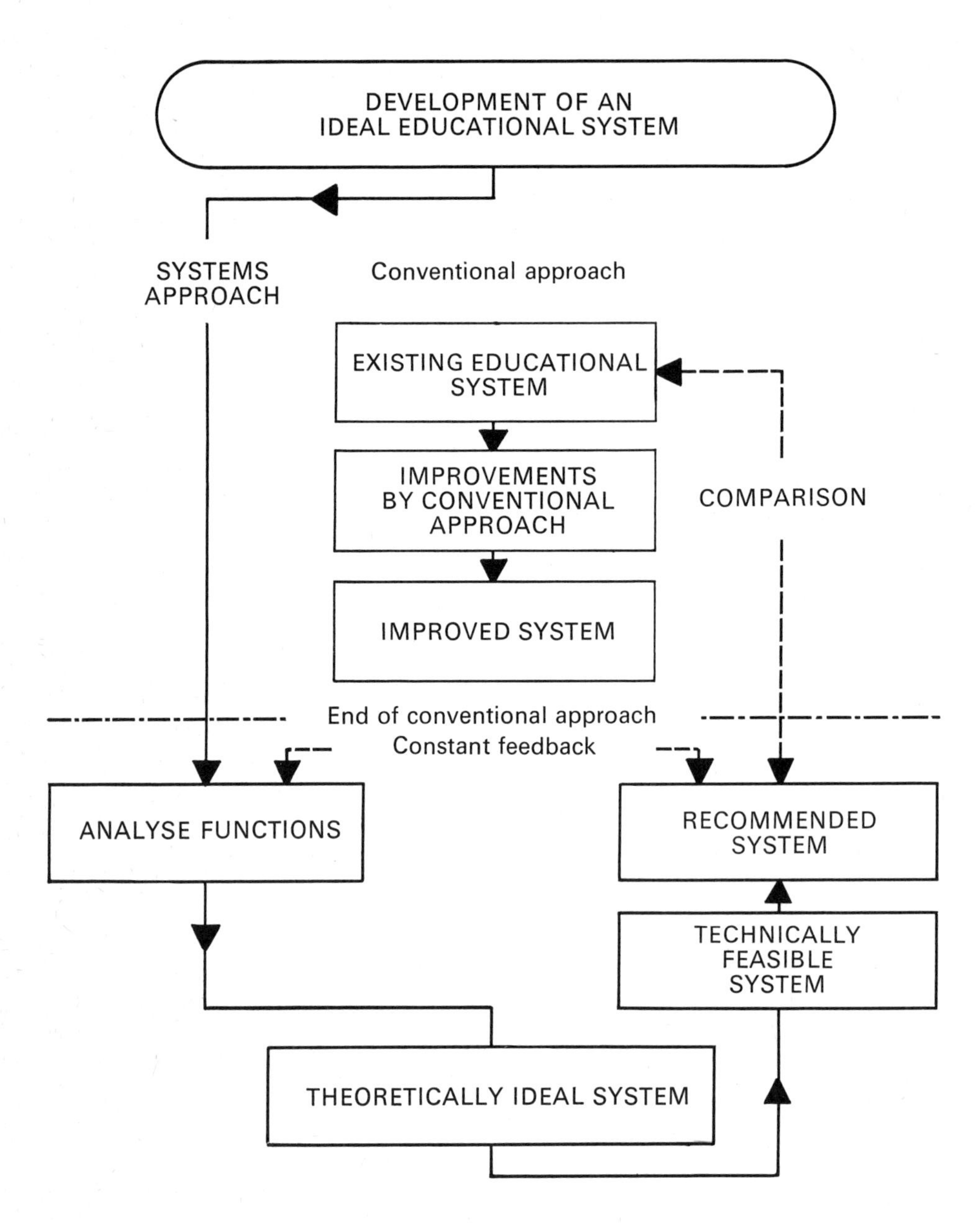

Different combinations of teaching aids

grammed instruction has become a regular feature of residential and non-residential training on work study and wage problems. The DGB Federal School created a programmed text introducing the basic features of the collective agreement which plays an essential part in German collective bargaining. This 65-frame programme proved so successful that circulation has now reached 18,000. It was supplemented by another one containing about 225 more frames and covering all the major legal aspects of collective agreements. The programme was mainly intended for members of bargaining committees at regional and plant levels. A test programme on works agreements, a supplementary feature of German labour law, has been tested and is under final revision. A 220-frame introduction to work measurement has recently been completed and tested. It is now available to unions and other users. It covers the modern range of work-measurement techniques, as well as the basic legal aspects of its application.

Originally, there was a great deal of resistance among trade union officials to the use of programmed instruction. It was considered as a kind of teaching which would leave no room for argument and discussion. But programmed instruction was never considered by its proponents as a general solution to teaching problems in trade unions. It was only considered as an efficient aid to the presentation of a given field of knowledge, with the guarantee of a firm degree of learning success. It cannot and will not abolish the role of the lecturer within a formal or informal discussion of different aspects of a subject. On the contrary, the use of programmed teaching provides a solid basis for discussion within a group and guarantees a common denominator which normally is not achieved by conventional classroom teaching. All programmed texts have been tested with 200 to 350 persons. Only after careful analysis and improvements, were they shaped into the final versions.

On the other hand, the programmes developed so far are more or less of linear type and rather long. It is therefore not easy to maintain the motivation and attention of readers and students for long periods of time, especially if these texts are not used within residential training, but on a part-time basis in evening courses. This has led to the concept of integrating teaching methods which are intended to break up long programmes into smaller ones to be filled with practical exercises, somewhat more complex tasks and room for discussion if used within a class or group. Initial tests have shown that a higher rate of success is obtained by integrating programmed teaching systematically into the whole teaching process than by using it in isolation.

Recently a new context model has been tested on a rather technical subject, work sampling, which is inceasingly applied in German industry. Trade union officers who are or who will be confronted with this technique have to be properly trained. The partially programmed work book is written in such a way that it can also be used for self-directed learning. The first test run of this programme proved very successful. The constant change of combinations of teaching aids and methods keeps motivation and interest alive and guarantees permanent participation of the students. The simulated case study can be given either:

- by filmstrips with sound, followed by
- 160 slides chosen at random by the lecturer,

FIGURE C. – MAIN AND SUBPHASES OF A COLLECTIVE BARGAINING GAME

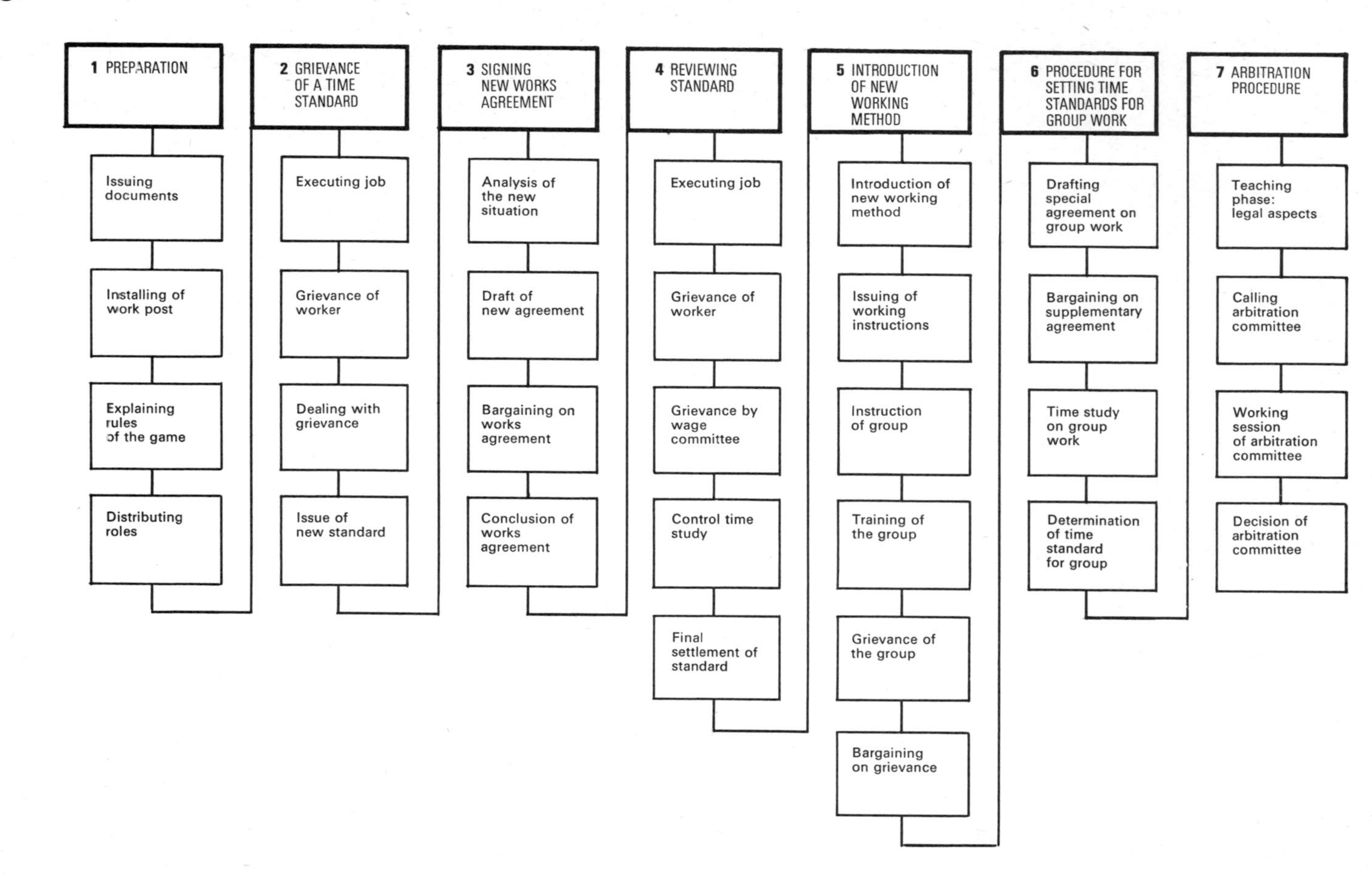

The instructor is always available to help

- by the simulation of a machine shop with machinery especially developed by R. Birkwald of IG Metall.

The programme ends with a test and contains a check list for practical follow-ups at the plant level. For training in the field of predetermined times, which becomes more and more important for setting standards, the IG Metall has developed a set of training materials, consisting of tools and materials, as well as a cassette tape recorder with the necessary instructions for several hundred exercises which carry the student through the rather complex subject. The teacher is always available to help the students in case of difficulties. The programme is interrupted by tests during which the questions are selected at random.

All the techniques mentioned are prefabricated and use different combinations of teaching aids and methods. They can be used by adequately trained teachers at local or regional levels. The rate of teaching success is greatly increased by the use of such integrated programmes. The German Productivity Centre (RKW) has supported most of these projects during their development.

Business games have become a regular feature of management training, sometimes in conjunction with a computer. Several years ago, the DGB Federal School tried to apply some of the basic principles of such business games to collective bargaining and work study problems. In the meantime, such a collective bargaining game has been standardised and refined. Figure C shows the major phases of the game, which has a practical work situation as a starting point. A practical work post for assembling electric appliances forms the basic situation. The following roles are distributed among the members of the course:

- a worker (later a three-men working group),
- a shop steward,
- a works council of three to five members,
- a wage committee according to the collective agreement,
- the foreman,
- the work study officer,
- the director or manager,
- the trade union secretary,
- the secretaries of the trade union and employer association.

A collective agreement, an existing works agreement and all the necessary data for the job are given. The data is given in such a way that the time allowed in the agreement for the piece rate is so short that the worker would not be able to achieve an acceptable level of earnings. After a short introductory teaching phase, the game is left to the discretion of participants. Naturally, each game leads to different intermediate results and, therefore, to ever-changing situations. The game ends with a conciliation procedure following the German Works Council law. The conciliation board is headed by an experienced judge with a broad practical background in this field. Since all the data used within the game are the result of the manoeuvring of the participants, a most efficient learning situation results.

This collective bargaining game presupposes a thorough knowledge of basic legal and work study subjects, as well as practical experience. It is therefore used only at a fairly advanced stage of teaching. It has been necessary to interrupt the game by short teaching phases and by discussions of intermediate results. For the participants in these games, this method proved to be extremely useful. The participation of students who play their proper roles and shift from one role to another is very active and their personal involvement in the game is quite intense. Discussions frequently touch on critical points. During one game, the "workers" of one department of the company concerned went on a wild-cat strike and made specific demands which forced the management and union representatives to come to terms.

Since the DGB Federal School tries to do pioneering work in the development of teaching methods, new experiments are always being prepared or tested. Experiences in the past few years indicate that the combination of adequate formal techniques such as programmed teaching, group discussions and integrated teaching methods such as context models and collective bargaining games are extremely valuable. This kind of teaching proves, in some cases, to be superior to the rather convential methods still used in the professional teaching of work study in West Germany. On the other hand, considering the high cost of trade union teaching and the short time available, it is necessary to provide the best means of achieving defined teaching objectives. These objectives must be chosen so that they directly foster the effiency of trade union officials in executing their proper functions. This kind of approach guarantees a very close-knit connection between trade union education and trade union action. At the same time, it provides competent negotiators and representatives of workers' interests at the plant level in a world in which sophisticated managers are becoming more and more predominant. ■

THREE RIVERS
PUBLIC LIBRARY DISTRICT
MINOOKA BRANCH
MINOOKA, IL 60447